Critical Issues in Lifespan Development
Examples for the Helping Professions

Randal E. Osborne
Susan J. Shapiro
William F. Browne
Carol S. Browne
Jane E. Vincent
Indiana University East

Allyn and Bacon
Boston London Toronto Sydney Tokyo Singapore

Copyright © 2000 by Allyn & Bacon
A Pearson Education Company
160 Gould Street
Needham Heights, Massachusetts 02494-2130

Internet: www.abacon.com

ISBN 0-205-27105-7

Printed in the United States of America

10 9 8 7 6 5 4 3 2 1   03 02 01 00

Table of Contents

NTRODUCTION

 **Psychology**

 **Education**

 **Health Care**

The authors of this text have written in response to the needs of students. Student with a diversity of majors take the lifespan development course at the undergraduate level, the texts have been written primarily by psychologists and the courses taught almost exclusively by psychology faculty. We think the major texts on the market are good, but few attempts have been made to apply the content of the lifespan course to the reality of working in the helping professions. This text represents our effort to bridge that gap. Given that the authors come from backgrounds in psychology, education, and health care, we represent a diversity of viewpoints and experience. From these viewpoints, then, we have written a text that illustrates how major concepts in lifespan development become relevant in and can be applied to the helping professions.

Many questions arise when contemplating the writing of a text. This effort proved to be no exception. It was our goal to write a text that would be beneficial in aiding students to apply the critical issues in lifespan development regardless of their major. For this reason, each of us had to consider how to step outside the mold of our own discipline and generate discussion and examples that were more global in nature. In addition to this consideration, decisions had to be made about how many examples to include, how many times to "revisit" the intragenerational family we created, how to aid students in developing the critical thinking skills necessary for working successfully in the helping professions, and how to accomplish all of these and still keep the book small and user-friendly. The text you are holding is the culmination of that decision making process.

It is our hope that you find the book both practical and stimulating. As you contemplate the profession you might want to pursue, it is important that you be able to analyze complex issues and problems in ways that are going to aid you in pursuing that profession. The critical thinking questions included within each chapter are designed to serve as a model for how professions approach issues of lifespan development. Additional critical thinking questions, and case analyses, then, are also included at the end of each chapter. Suggested readings are included to provide additional resources for students to pursue issues they find to be of particular interest.

Much of an individual's understanding of his or her own development is tempered by that very development. How we think and feel about who we are is intricately intertwined with what we have experienced. In other words, our assessment of our own development cannot be completely removed from the very developmental process we have experienced. This is a critical consideration in the helping professions. One cannot look at a particular case, say a child brought to the emergency room with unusual burns on his arm, and simply treat the outward problem. In order to provide the best possible care to that individual, we have to know many things. Is he allergic to any medication? Has he been brought to the hospital in the past? If so, was it under similar circumstances? Do the burns appear to be self-inflicted? Are there any signs that would indicate that the burns are the result of abuse?

Although the answers to these questions do not alter the medical treatment that is provided, per se, they should provide insights to us as professionals about what other care this individual should receive. It is this model of learning, "to ask the next question", that has guided our development of this text. Each of the professions included have particular questions they would want to ask about the same case. As the reader will discover, the answers one receives about a case and the recommendations one would make about what to do are only as "good" as the questions the professional thinks to ask. The questions one thinks to ask, however, are often influenced by one's personal perspective. If a doctor, for example, assumes that reports of child abuse are greatly exaggerated, he or she might be less likely to ask questions about the "unusual" nature of the burns than a doctor who believes that abuse occurs often. One's perspective, therefore, becomes an important part of one's professional approach.

We adopted a particular perspective in the development of this text and it is important that you, as a reader, understand our reasons for adopting this perspective. Many assumptions are made when one considers a lifespan perspective on human development. It is our opinion that a lifespan perspective of development should take the lead of Baltes, Reese, and Lipsitt (1980) in making five assumptions about the lifespan. This text, then, uses these assumptions as underlying themes that weave themselves through the chapters, the case examples, and the critical reflection exercises we have included. The lifespan perspective assumes that:

Development is a lifelong process. This approach moves beyond the traditional emphasis on childhood and adolescent development and assumes that development is a dynamic and lifelong process. Critical factors and issues affect development. Rather than looking at development within stages or phases as isolated events, development should be studied as a dynamic, lifelong, multi-directional process. Studying core concepts and issues and then discussing examples from Education, Health care profession, and Psychology will not only reinforce readers' understanding of the lifelong nature of development but will also enhance students' abilities to relate the material to their own disciplines.

Development must be viewed in a historical context. Development does not occur in a vacuum and, as such, the historical influences of the time will have an impact. A lifespan approach to development considers the impact of such factors as family, economic conditions, and culture. Of course, differing factors may be relevant given the particular discipline the student is studying. The interdisciplinary nature of this text with examples from each of the three areas illustrates this historical importance.

Development can take multiple directions. Traditional views of development tended to assume that developmental changes were always "additive" in direction. This view holds that persons will experience incremental changes toward more mature levels of functioning in all areas as they develop. A lifespan approach, however, assumes that humans develop through a series of starts and stops, gains and losses, positives, and negatives. Factors such as health, education, self-certainty, self-concept, and self-esteem are dynamic and fluid. As such, they will wax and wane right along with the events in the individual's life and how the individual experiencing them is interpreting those events.

As individuals progress across their lifespan (maturing as some have said "from womb to tomb"), there will be many peaks and valleys to endure. Are we truly finished needing constant care when we mature from the overwhelming dependency of infancy to the increased independence of middle childhood? Although many of us would prefer not to ponder such issues, will we ourselves need such constant care again due to disease or illness in old age? Students will gain a more integrated understanding of these complex issue as they see the multiple influences on development from the three perspectives.

This lifespan approach also assumes that multiple factors, both internal and external to the person, must be considered if an accurate view of development is to be possible. Both maturation and learning have been shown to contribute to the development of individuals. Each of these disciplines is particularly attuned to the internal and environmental influences on development and it is critical that students in these disciplines have this reinforced within the context of studying lifespan development. A complete understanding of development necessitates an analysis of both the internal (maturational or biological) factors that influence development as well as the external (social, environmental or learning) variables that impinge upon the individual. Cultural differences are also extremely important within this framework. What is "acceptable" treatment (treatment being defined broadly to include medical treatment, acceptable parental discipline strategies, educational methods, etc.) of others may differ dramatically from culture to culture.

4 **Development in any phase of life can best be understood in context of the lifespan**. This, in essence, is the heart of the lifespan approach to understanding development. For too long, development has been broken into ages or phases and researchers would expose particular ages or phases to microscopic analysis. Although such an analysis results in a detailed understanding of the specific age or phase being addressed, it does little to shed light on the interconnections among these ages or phases. Certainly the behavioral choices that an adolescent makes are determined, in part, by earlier experiences. These current choices will also, in some fashion, influence future options.

Let us return to the case of the child with the unusual burns on his arm. Without addressing this child within the context of the lifespan, we would be unable to realistically understand the complete picture. Let us say that we discover the burns are self-inflicted. Could we truly understand the impact of this on the child's development without considering what previous experiences might have led to such behaviors and what implications such actions have for the future development of this child? The goal of this text, then, is to help you, as a student in the lifespan development course, develop critical thinking and analysis skills that will aid you in applying course content to the analysis of cases from a variety of the helping professions. In this fashion, we believe you will have a more sophisticated understanding of not only lifespan development but also of how the issues in lifespan development relate to the professions you and your student colleagues may be pursuing.

earning Objectives:

Before moving on to a description of the intragenerational family that we will visit several times throughout the pages of this text, it would be wise to establish the major learning objectives for the text. After you have reached the last pages of this text and have completed the critical thinking exercises included, you will understand the importance of viewing lifespan development in context of the helping professions. The following list summarizes the concepts that will be illustrated within the examples used in the text. As a reader, then, you should be able to discuss and develop well-informed answers to questions about each one.

- **The interaction of physical, cognitive, personal, and social development that gives each period of the lifespan, and each individual, a distinctive and coherent quality.**

- **There is both a universality and an individuality to our development.**

- **We are individuals, becoming more diverse with age.**

- **Development proceeds in multiple directions, entailing at times gains, at other times losses, and at still other times just change.**

- **With age, behavior becomes more complex and organized, more differentiated and integrated.**

  There is both continuity and discontinuity in development.

  There is both qualitative and quantitative change.

  There is both consistency and inconsistency with age-mates.

  There is both stability and change in development over time.

- **Nature (maturation) and nurture (learning) truly interact.**

- **Because of learning, variation is possible.**

- **Maturation sets limits beyond which development cannot progress.**

- **Early experiences influence but do not determine later outcomes.**

- **Development is aided by stimulation.**

- **We are active in our own development.**

- **The family plays a central role in guiding and directing individual development.**

- **Development has multiple causes.**

  Normative maturational events - a biological clock

  Normative social events - a social clock

  Historical events - cohort effects

  Nonnormative events - unique, individualistic events

- **Development is a lifelong process and thus is best viewed from a lifespan perspective.**

- **We develop in a cultural and historical context; our knowledge of development is therefore culture bound and time bound. Much remains to be learned about development.**

 If you would like to use resources on the World Wide Web as you explore Lifespan Development, we have made a list of resources available at:

http://www.iue.indiana.edu/psych/lifespan/index.html.

The ntragenerational amily

Contemporary families are becoming increasingly complex. As such, many of the issues in lifespan development arise within the context of everyday family life. Individuals experience many changes within the context of the family, or in response to crises that the family must confront and attempt to resolve. We will consider critical issues in lifespan development occasionally by looking at a specific individual. In other cases, we will underscore the complexity of these issues by considering them from the perspective of a diverse and extended fictional intragenerational family. Since we will revisit this family several times throughout our trek across the lifespan, we will introduce them to the reader now.

Grandparents:

Gene Tran

age 68. Recently widowed, Gene is attempting to "redefine" himself without his wife of 41 years. Gene, a foreperson for the state highway department, is the father of Thomas Tran.

Virginia Long

age 66. Virginia has taught private piano lessons for over twenty years. She seems agitated and depressed most of the time. She has been diagnosed with Alzheimer's Disease and is currently suffering the middle stages of the disorder. She is Susan Tran's mother and Robert's wife.

Robert Long

age 67. Robert recently retired after forty years with the same manufacturing company. Although he and Virginia had made many plans to buy a motor home and travel once he retired, her Alzheimer's Disease has created a different pattern of retirement than either of them had planned. He is Susan Tran's father and Virginia's husband.

Parents:

Thomas Tran

age 40. Thomas is an upper level manager for a series of electronics stores. Of Asian decent, he prides himself on being culturally diverse and multiculturally aware. Thomas is the husband of Susan Tran.

Susan Tran

age 38. Susan teaches second grade for the local district and prides herself on her involvement with the Parent Teachers Organization. Susan is the wife of Thomas Tran.

Children:

Austin Tran

age 18. Austin enjoys being the "big brother" but is concerned about how his status in the family might be affected by his move to college.

Jessica Tran

age 14. Jessica is adjusting to recent changes brought on by adolescence. Although she loves her parents dearly, she expresses frustration over their recent battles concerning her attempts to secure increased autonomy.

Kyle Tran

age 10. Susan and Thomas describe Kyle as "generally a well-behaved boy." He is currently encountering some difficulties in school and was recently diagnosed with Attention Deficit Disorder (ADD).

CHAPTER 1

METHODS & THEORY IN STUDYING LIFESPAN DEVELOPMENT

Human behavior was primarily the field of inquiry of philosophers until the 19th century. Now it is the concern of several of the biological sciences a well as the social sciences. It is truly a multidisciplinary field. Developmental psychology is the largest of the disciplines and is concerned with identifying and explaining the changes that each individual undergoes across the life span. In addition to psychologists, many biologists, sociologists, anthropologists, educators, nurses, physicians, historians and others have made major contributions to the field of study. Today those who study human development are referred to by the term developmentalists.

Simply stated, development refers to systematic changes in the individual that occur between conception and death. Implicit to the developmentalist is the idea that change is orderly or patterned and that temporary or transitory change is to be excluded in the development of theory. The study of human development is in some ways no different from any other field of study. One must form hypotheses and scientifically test them.

The scientific method is used by modern-day psychologists to collect information and draw conclusions about how people develop. Although the scientific method comes in various forms, there are always the requirements that the researchers be objective and that their theories be supported by data. The scientific method is more of an attitude or value than a method and it therefore helps to protect the scientific community and society from flawed reasoning.

Critical Issue - The Functions of Theories

Theories perform many functions, but two of the most important functions are that they: (1) organize and give meaning to facts, and (2) guide research. Developmental theories most often disagree on two issues: (1) which facts or concepts are most important and (2) the significance of the relationships among concepts. While there is no one best theory, theories are important because they act as filters to screen out some facts and impose structure on those they consider. Therefore, theory influences the questions asked, the methods used and ultimately which results are found.

Alfred Baldwin (1980) reflects that, ideally, a theory should not only be logical but also supply clear definitions. A theory should make specific prediction about behaviors that are verifiable. Furthermore, a theory should be falsifiable. That is, it should be possible to prove that the theory does not make accurate predictions. Finally, a developmental theory should call attention to changes in types of behavior that occur during development. None of the theories discussed in developmental textbooks possess all the characteristics of an ideal theory. However, each needs to be studied because each one has made it possible to organize facts and has stimulated considerable research since its inception.

②Critical Issue - Putting Theories into Perspective

All theories are concerned with identifying and explaining the processes involved in human behavior and development. In addition, they all assume that there are predictable and regular patterns to growth and development. The theories differ in terms of the aspects of development on which they focus and the nature of the explanation offered for any given behavior or process.

Theories of development attempt to explain four characteristics of age-related change:

1.) Orderliness

2.) Directionality

3.) Cumulativeness and

4.) Increasing differentiation and integration.

Most theories fall into two broad categories: **mechanistic and organismic.**

Mechanistic theories use the machine as a basic metaphor. Several corollaries of this view, when applied to human development, include the beliefs that:

- The infant's mind is a blank slate

- The organism is inherently at rest and that behavior therefore occurs only in response to external stimulation

- The child is passive

- Understanding of the world is a true reflection of an objective reality that is independent of the individual or naive realism

- Development is a continuous acquisition of knowledge and experience. Skinner's behavior-learning theory argues that behavior and development are a function of learning experiences.

The basic metaphor for **organismic theories** is the organism. Several corollaries specific to this view are:

1) The child is active

2) **Constructionism**, or the belief that the world cannot be known objectively; instead knowledge of it is constructed by the individual

3) Development is a discontinuous progression through a series of qualitatively different stages; and

4) Development is determined by the interaction between genetic maturation and experience. Piaget's theory states that the child is a constructionist and development consists of qualitatively different ways of knowing the world.

③ Critical Issue - The Implications of Theoretical Perspectives

Developmental theorists differ on five very basic issues:

1 Is the human organism good, neutral or inherently bad?

Early views of human development saw the individual as inherently bad (doctrine of original sin), as inherently good (doctrine of innate purity), or as neither bad nor good (doctrine of tabula rasa). Today's theories include these ideas, however, now theorists emphasize either the positive or the negative aspects. Understanding this is important because it helps us to see how theoretical content is influenced, hypothesis formed, and certain research questions are generated.

2 Is nature (biological forces) or nurture (environmental forces) the primary influence on human development?

This is one of the oldest controversies. The question simply asks whether genetics or environment is the primary influence on ones development. Today most developmentalists subscribe to what is often called the interactionist position (Anastasi, 1958). They want to know how nature and nurture work together to influence traits and capacities.

3 Is the human organism actively involved in the developmental process? Are we passively influenced by social and biological forces?

Organismic theories assure that change is from within the individual structures existing inside the organism that create a foundation for and control development. Therefore, we are viewed as active, purposeful beings that make sense of our world and determine much of our own learning. In contrast, mechanistic theories focus on the relationship between environmental inputs and behavioral outputs. Change is a passive reaction to the environment.

4 Is development continuous or discontinuous?

The continuous view of development regards development as a cumulative process of adding on more of the same types of skills with which he organism began. A discontinuous view assumes that new and different ways of interpreting and responding to the world emerge at particular time periods. These latter approaches assume that stages are present in development and qualitative changes characterize the particular stages or time periods in the life span. Some contemporary changes are characteristic of human development and may alternate with one another.

5 Do humans follow similar or different developmental paths?

Theorists also often disagree on whether developmental changes are individualistic or universal. Discontinuous (stage) theorists assure that the stages are universal. Other theorists argue that developmental change varies from culture to culture and is much less universal.

Critical Issue - How Do We Measure What Interests Us?

For research to be meaningful, the data that investigators collect must be **reliable** and **valid**. A research method is reliable if it produces consistent, replicable results. The method is valid if it measures precisely what it claims to measure. An instrument must be reliable and measure consistently before it can be valid. However, being reliable is not sufficient for validity.

As an example, we might have a technique that measures a person's foot. Except for small changes based on weather, etc. we would expect to get relatively the same result each time we use this technique to measure an adult's foot. If we do receive the same result each time we measure the same adult's foot, we can claim that our measurement technique is reliable (consistent). But is it valid? It depends on what we are claiming the technique measures. If we claim that the technique measures shoe size, then it would appear to be a valid measure. However, what if we are claiming that the technique measures "intelligence?" Then we would be hard pressed to convince someone else that our technique provides a valid measurement.

The most common methods of collecting data on human development include self-report measures such as interviews, questionnaires, case studies, and clinical procedures. Data can also be collected through direct observations that are made either in the natural environment or in structured laboratory settings.

Naturalistic observation is a valuable method that often uses time-sampling techniques although observer bias can interfere with scientific objectivity and thus must be carefully avoided, by checking observer reliability. Another problem is that the observer's presence can cause people to behave differently. In naturalistic observation it is difficult to determine what the actual causes of behavior are and thus naturalistic observation often provides a starting point for research on causes.

In the **interview method**, the researcher asks a series of carefully selected questions. A structured interview makes it possible to compare answers directly because each participant is asked the same questions and the questions are asked in the same order. Although it is hard to know whether answers are honest and accurate, interviews can be designed to challenge subjects to answer accurately by posing problems. A variation is the clinical method, in which the researcher asks varying questions according to how the person responds. This method yields protocols such as those of Piaget in his studies of cognitive development. Problems with this method include difficulty in comparing responses of different people, plus the increased possibility that the researcher's subjectivity can affect the results.

Another variation of the interview method is the **case study,** in which an individual or case is assessed repeatedly and extensively through observation, testing, or interviews, as in Freud's work. Case studies are a rich source of information and are particularly useful when what is to be studied is extremely rare or other methods might be unethical.

Let us say we are interested in gathering information about the characteristics of women who have flown on NASA Space Shuttle missions. It would not make sense to create surveys and collect data from a random sample of women. Instead, we want to intensively investigate just those women who have served in that role. A case study, then, would allow us to collect rich data on just the individuals we are interested in examining. With case studies, there are problems with accuracy and generalizability to other people, as well as difficulties in comparing results from different cases.

The experimental method is considered to be objective and also allows the researcher to assess causes for behavior. Typically, the participants are sorted into groups who receive different treatments, thus establishing an independent variable. In turn measuring the dependent variable shows the researcher whether the different treatments caused an effect.

Let us say that we are interested in determining if ingesting caffeine before a quiz will improve performance. We would randomly divide our students into two groups. The first group will be given coffee with caffeine. The second group will be given decaffeinated coffee. Neither group knows whether they are receiving caffeine. Then we measure performance on the quiz. An independent variable is what is manipulated between the groups and a dependent variable is an outcome that is measured. So, in this example, the independent variable (what is manipulated) is the presence of caffeine (it is also just the difference between what is done to the two groups). The dependent variable (the outcome that is measured) would be quiz scores. The reason that this variable is called "dependent" is that we assume that quiz score performance "depends" on whether or not the students ingested caffeine.

To be confident of the causes, researchers strive for **experimental control**. This includes treating the subjects the same in all ways other than the independent variable (that is why both groups in the example above were given coffee to drink.) The groups are made as much alike as possible through **random assignment** (when we let chance divide our students in the above example into two groups, we were using the concept of random assignment). We use random assignment to make sure that it is as likely as possible that there are not significant differences between our groups before the study even starts. If we told our students, for example, that we wanted to test the impact of caffeine on performance and had them volunteer to receive or not receive caffeine, that might bias our data. Perhaps there is already something different about people who want to ingest caffeine versus those who do not.

One recurring criticism is that laboratory experiments may be artificial, and so researchers often conduct field experiments in natural settings such as home or school, as in contrast, quasi-experiments take advantage of naturally occurring independent variables rather than experimentally controlled ones. But it is difficult to assess causation versus correlation.

Measuring developmental "change" requires special research designs. A research design in which groups of participants of different ages are studied at the same point in time is an example of the **cross-sectional** comparison. But, researchers are often mislead on changes in development since factors other than developmental change can influence the findings in cross-sectional research. Some of these problems are eliminated in **longitudinal** comparisons, but new problems are created. With this technique the same people are studied at different points across time, thus allowing more of a look at individual differences in development; but such projects are costly and very time-consuming. Loss of subjects can produce a nonrepresentative sample. And there is the cohort effect or cross-generational problem that our world is continuously changing at the same time that the subjects are developing.

Thus, the **longitudinal-sequential design** combines the first two methods. This method saves time and money, and it also provides the clearest information about developmental change. A recent modification of the longitudinal approach, called the microgenetic design is becoming popular because it offers unique insights into how development takes place. Researchers track change while it occurs, observing frequently from the time it begins until **it stabilizes.**

The **generalizability of research** findings across different cultures is also an issue, and thus **cross-cultural comparisons** assess whether findings are universal or culturally relative. Culture-specific patterns of behavior are also important to an understanding of human development.

⑤ Critical Issue - Ethical Considerations in Developmental Research

In studying human development, the issue of research ethics is always present. The most basic guideline is that all subjects must be protected from potential mental or physical harm. Two important principles are (1) **informed consent** or written consent to participate (children by age 7 should also sign a consent form) and (2) **right of privacy**: subjects must be assured that highly personal information they may provide will be kept entirely private. Researchers can use the information "collectively" but can not report individually unless specific permission has been given.

With children in particular, the investigator must bear in mind that the child's rights come first, that the responsibility for maintaining ethical practices rests with the investigator, that the child must be informed and can refuse to participate at any point, that parental consent is required, and that no operation can be employed that may harm the child either physically or psychologically. When in doubt, and since it is always necessary to weigh the possible benefits of the research against the potential risks to the participants, research is typically reviewed and evaluated by professional committees in making a decision about whether to proceed. These considerations apply to all research involving human participants. But, many questions remain as to what is ethical in research. For example questioning:

- whether children can be exposed to situations in which socially inappropriate behavior will occur,

- whether asking children about parental discipline is an invasion of privacy,

- whether subjects can be deceived in the course of research, whether naturalistic observation can occur without informing the participants, and

- whether verbal punishment can be used.

Research Question

A major contribution of Piaget's theory is his view of children as naturally curious beings who actively explore and try to understand. His theory is the most detailed and integrated version of cognitive development. Critics of his theory point out that one difficulty with his theory is the timing of his stages. Another problem is the implication that development occurs abruptly, in stages, rather than continuously. Finally, Piaget's theory has been criticized as being merely descriptive of cognitive development rather than explanation.

What research can you find to address these criticisms and fill the gaps?

Recent research indicates that preoperational children are less egocentric than Piaget supposed. They sometimes take others points of view, although not always. Piaget may have also underestimated the peroperational child's causal reasoning. For example, various researchers have found that conservation problems can be taught to preoperational children by methods such as identity training. How could you find out if reversibility and compensation are necessary for conservation?

onclusions

Development refers to those changes that occur in association with increasing chronological age or the passing of time. Change does not occur without purpose. Developmentalists assume that change will lead the individual to attain his/her potential as a unique, fully functioning human being. Change is studied by a variety of methods and research designs. Often more than one method is used to gather data. Each method and design has its own unique reliability and validity. Research is usually found to be based on a particular theory (ies). As yet no one theory best describes human development. The one thing common to all research and investigation into human development is the strict adherence to ethical practices and the presentation of human subjects.

aper Topics

- John Lock and Jean-Jacques Rousseau had very different perspectives on development. Compare and contrast their position and show how recent theory has evolved for these.

- Choose either Skinner's <u>Walden Two</u> or Neil's <u>Summer Hill</u> and analyze the contents with regard to parenting, education, health or any area which may impact you as a professional or citizen.

- Choose one of the major theorists discussed in your text. Research the individual's background and identify specifics that may have influenced their theory. For example, Freud's theory has been criticized on the basis that it was designed around problems of sexually repressed, upper class Victorians.

Suggested Readings

Kagan, J. (1984*). The nature of the child*. New York: Basic Books.

Kessen, W. (Ed.), & Mussen, P. H. (Series Ed.). 1983. *Handbook of child psychology: Vol. 1. History, theory and methods*. New York: Wiley.

Miller, P. H. (1993). *Theories of developmental psychology* (3rd ed.). New York: W. H. Freeman and Company.

Seitz, V. (1988). Methodology. In M. H. Bornstein & M. E. Lamb (Eds.), *Developmental Psychology: An advanced textbook* (2nd ed.) (pp. 51-84).Hillsdale, NJ: Earlbaum.

Thomas, R. M. (Ed.) (1990). The encyclopedia of human development and education. *Theory, research, and studies*. Oxford: Pergamon Press.

xercise 1
Research Methods

Read each of the following two examples and identify

1) variables (e.g. independent, dependent, etc.)

2) method (e.g. experimental, interview, case study, etc.)

3) design (cross-sectional/longitudinal, etc.)

4) questions concerning reliability and/or validity

Researchers set up lab to look much like a family home. Pairs of one-year olds, two-year olds and three-year olds were brought into the setting and allowed to play in the family room while two adults had a conversation in an adjacent room. One of each pair experienced a "warm" atmosphere in which the adult conversation was friendly and calm. The second child in each pair experiences a situation in which the adults began to argue and shout and make loud noises. The research hypothesis was that the quality of adult interaction would effect the children's emotional reaction while playing with a familiar companion. The results of the study showed the even short periods of time spent with intense adult anger can create negative emotions and antisocial behavior.

A group of researchers was interested in whether the amount of positive vs. negative reinforcement received by a group of adults in an adult day care facility was relative to their satisfaction with life in general. Through a two way observation window the researchers were able to view the adults in a recreation room. The researchers developed a "Satisfaction Towards Life Scale," consisting of twenty open ended questions. Each adult was asked the twenty questions and the answers were recorded. For seven days the researchers observed the adults noting any positive or negative exchanges between guests, staff and/or other clients and each adult. Results of the study supported the hypothesis that the more positive or negative the responses to an individual the more positive or negative the response to others. A post test with the Satisfaction Towards Life Scale showed a similar result. The research concluded the reinforcement history of the individual is directly related to their satisfaction, and is no doubt universal.

xercise 2
Theory

Think of several people that you know.

Which theory or theories best explain(s) each of these individuals.

You might choose characteristics, needs, or behavior as your focus for analysis.

xercise 3
Questions

List four to six questions about research and developmental theory.

Find several people (3-4) who work in service oriented professions (e.g. nurse, social worker, teacher, counselor, psychologist, etc.).

Make an appointment to interview each of them (one-half to one hour). Explain that you want to discuss the role of theory in their profession.

Ask each of them the questions you have generated. You might want to ask them which theory of development they feel best aids them as a professional.

Compare the responses from each professional to see if you find any consistent similarities or any specific differences. After your interviews and your analysis of the responses, reflect whether your theoretical viewpoint has changed. If so, why?

xercise 4
Developmental Theories: A Research Problem

Assume a researcher has developed a scale to measure internality vs. externality (IE) and wants to use the scale to test the hypothesis that internally oriented individuals are more empathetic than externally oriented individuals.

1) What problems might she be faced with?

2) What type of design(s) might she use?

3) What role would theory play?

4) What possible ethical considerations might she face?

xercise 5
Developmental Theories: Point of View

Examine the position of the major developmental theories:

For each theory choose whether it is:

Organismic (O) or Mechanistic (M)
Continuous (C) or Discontinuous (D)
and whether
Nature (NA) or Nurture (NU) or both (B) are important.

Theory	Organismic	Mechanistic
Behaviorism		
Information Processing		
Ethology		
Piaget's Cognitive Developmental Theory Psychodynamic Perspectives		

Theory	Discontinuous	Continuous
Behaviorism		
Information Processing		
Ethology		
Piaget's Cognitive Developmental Theory Psychodynamic Perspectives		

Theory	Nature	Both Important	Nurture
Behaviorism			
Information Processing			
Ethology			
Piaget's Cognitive Developmental Theory Psychodynamic Perspectives			

CHAPTER 2

GENES AND THE ENVIRONMENT

Physical maturation and psychological development are shaped by biological factors such as genetics. As the individual matures, the influence of biology becomes less dominant and experiential history has more influence on the current characteristics of the individual. Still, there is never a point in the development process where both biological and environmental factors do not play a part.

 ## Critical Issue – Nature

While nature is often equated with heredity, there are many biological factors which determine future development. The genetic structure inherited from parents can be modified by mutation and recombination of the available genes. Influences from the mother's internal environment and the external world can limit or distort biological development. For example: The presence of alcohol in the mother's blood stream can enter the fetus through the placenta. Alcohol can slow and distort development of the cells in the fetus. Neural cells in the brain may not migrate to appropriate locations. The outcome is a biological impairment in nervous system functioning.

Genetic

Genes are a controlling factor in physical development. They control characteristics from hair color to personality, to a predisposition to some types of illness. While genetics is not as simple as the recessive and dominant genes proposed by Mendel, knowing about genetic structure does allow some predictions about appearance, behavior, and health.

Congenital

Sometimes there are characteristics that appear at birth, that may or may not be genetic. Some are due to a prenatal influence such as maternal illness or a teratogen. It may be difficult to determine the real cause of such characteristics since there are few ways to observe the earliest stages of development.

While congenital problems are not necessarily genetic, they are biological and the fact that they are present at birth increases their influence on future behavior.

 ## Critical Issue - Nurture

The influence of the environment

Human beings grow in a complex environment that includes the physical and social world around them as well as the internal mental world that they create for themselves. It is easy to forget how ever-present the environment is.

We often take the environment for granted, but it does change who we are. Not only do factors such as weather effect psychological states, as is seen in seasonal affective disorder (SAD), but they may also be related to the predisposition for mental illness or the prevalence of behaviors. For example: schizophrenia is more commonly found in individuals born during winter months and more patents are requested by individuals living in temperate climates.

Teratogens

Teratogens are an example of the influence of the external environment on the internal environment or physical body. Common teratogens include: drugs taken by the mother during or before pregnancy, environmental toxins, and maternal illness during or before pregnancy.

Learning

Much of what is referred to as nurture can also be called learning. As development takes place, the social environment encourages some behaviors and discourages others. The behaviors may be anything from the way you hold your body to the thoughts that you use to explain your world or the attitudes you express.

 # Critical Issue – The Interaction Between Nature and Nurture

It is interesting to discuss the individual effects of nature and nurture. Both influence development in many ways. It may be a matter of one having more influence in a particular area or on a single individual, but it is typically the interaction of genetically programed structures with an ever-changing environment that makes you who you are today.

 # Critical Issue - Sensitive Periods

Development takes place throughout life, but within the lifespan there a periods of time that are more sensitive to environmental influences. These are sometimes called sensitive or critical periods. When cells are dividing rapidly they are more easily effected by external influences that disrupt the normal process of development or impair the development of a particular structure or ability.

Sensitive periods are most visible in the earliest stages of development as at this time there is rapid change and growth and effects on single cells or single abilities can have lifelong effects. The human organism begins a single cell. As this cell divides, the individual cells begin to take on specific shapes and functions. Some cells become nervous tissue. Others become bones or muscle. If something disrupts development when a particular structure is changing, it may not be able to recover. In the fetus this can result in missing limbs, incomplete hearts, and a variety of problems in nervous system structures and connections.

Even later in life there appear to be times when specific skills must be learned if they are to be used later. An eye that gets distorted information from an irregularity in the lens may never be able to focus on lines in a particular orientation, resulting in an astigmatism. A child who does not learn language early in life may not be able to use language fluently as an adult.

 # Critical Issue - Genetic Disorders and Ethical Decisions

Although there is increased understanding about the causes of genetic disorders, it is still not possible to change genetic structure enough to make these disorders disappear. It is increasingly possible to discover genetic problems early in development rather than waiting until the symptoms of the disorder appear, (Sometimes late in life, as in Huntington's Chorea). Knowing of the potential for a problem to occur creates emotional and ethical problems for parents and medical professionals. Medical advances and personal choice make it possible to decide whether or not to conceive a child or to let a fetus with a genetic disorder live. There are religious, medical and personal factors which must be weighed while making these decisions.

esearch uestion

One of the most interesting studies done in the past few years is the Minnesota Twins Study (Bouchard, 1987; Bouchard, Lyken, McGue, Segal, & Tellegen, 1990). Twins raised together and twins separated at birth were located and given an extensive series of physical and psychological tests and interviews. The researchers were interested in the types of characteristics accounted for by genetic similarity as opposed to the effects of experience. While expected similarities were found in such areas and general intelligence and predisposition to some types of illness, there were often surprising similarities in occupations and hobbies, fears, and coping strategies. It is likely that there is a genetic influence on more than just physically visible characteristics.

How might you go about finding evidence that parent's similarities to their children have biological as well as environmental causes?

onclusion:

Nature and nurture both play a role in who we are and how we develop. To leave one or the other out will inhibit our ability to understand human behavior and development.

Popular interpretations of the influence of heredity or the environment often go to far, placing blame and limiting the possibility of individual differences. Just because your parents have a particular problem or ability, does not mean that you will be identical to them. Each individual inherits his or her own mix of genes, and puts them to use in a different environment. Inheritance should not be a reason for limiting opportunities and environment is not an excuse for inappropriate behavior.

Learning about your biological inheritance can provide insight into your behavior, just as observing your environment can explain a great deal about what you do.

aper opics

1. Look for information on the Human Genome Project. Take one of the possible uses of the information that will be available when the project is completed. Discuss the psychological, social, and/or biological implications of this information.

2. Find an article in a popular magazine or newspaper that refers to a genetic issue. Locate the original research, or research on the topic discussed, in a professional journal. Compare the two articles.

3. Do you feel that the information in the research article has been interpreted accurately and fairly?

4. There are many folk sayings that reflect a belief in the influence of nature or nurture. Choose one of these sayings and write a paper providing evidence supporting or discounting the saying.

Examples include:

- Blood is thicker than water.

- Spare the rod and spoil the child.

- An acorn does not fall far from the tree.

uggested eadings

Bouchard, T.J. Jr. (1987). *Information about the Minnesota center for twin and adoption research*. Minneapolis, MN: University of Minnesota Press.

Bouchard, T.J. Jr., Lyken, D.T., McGue, M., Segal, N.L., & Tellegen, A. (1990). Sources of human psychological differences: The Minnesota study of twins reared apart. *Science, 250*, 223-228.

Ploman, Robert (1990*). Nature and nurture: An introduction to human behavioral genetics*. Belmont, CA: Brooks/Cole.

xercise 1

Nature or Nurture or Both

Professor Svenson has just won a Nobel prize for her contributions to Physics. List factors which could have come from her genetic endowment and factors which could have come from her environment which made this accomplishment possible.

Sasha is the best student in his fifth grade class. Although his clothes are often dirty or torn, he is well behaved and attentive, always does his assignments and is polite to the teacher and other students. Sasha's father was a construction worker who left when Sasha was three years old. His mother is a waitress at the local diner. She did not finish high school after she became pregnant with Sasha. Describe factors which could have come from his genetic endowment and factors which could have come from his environment which could determine Sasha's school performance.

Lila has blond hair and beautiful blue eyes, just like her mother. Her father has brown hair and green eyes. Shortly before Lila was born, Lila's mother began to bleach her brown hair and got colored contacts to change her brown eyes. Describe factors which could have come from her genetic endowment and factors which could have come from her environment which determine Lila's hair and eye color.

Brandy is 12 years old. When she was born the doctor diagnosed Down's Syndrome. Her eyes and face have the characteristics typical of Down's Syndrome and she is short for her age. Brandy's parents have encouraged her and worked with her. She is now in a normal classroom and is doing work at an average level for a child her age. Describe factors which could have come from her genetic endowment and factors which could have come from her environment which determine her current abilities.

Ted is 6 foot 5 inches tall and very athletic. His father is 6 feet tall and is a marathon runner. His mother is 5 foot 8 inches tall and is a basketball coach at the local high school. Ted has become the star of his high school basketball team. Describe factors which could have come from his genetic endowment and factors which could have come from his environment which made this accomplishment possible.

xercise 2

Interpreting Research

Sit down with someone you do not know well. Look for things that you have in common such as: a favorite color or food, a way of doing something, things that you find funny or frightening, the way you respond to stressful situations, your preferences in men/women, the type of class that you do well in, habits (good or bad), types of exercise, children's names .

Compare the similarities that you found to the similarities found between twins raised in different environments through the Minnesota twin study.

Do you think that there is evidence for or against genetic involvement in such things as personality traits based on your observations and the twin research?

xercise 3
The social effects of physical differences

Albinism is a congenital disorder that results in a lack of the pigment melanin in the skin, eye, and other tissues. Albino individuals can be found in any ethnic group. Ben is an albino child born into an African American family. His skin is very pale and his eyes are more yellow than brown. His hair is kinky, but a very pale tan in color.

How might this physical condition influence Ben's life?

What problems and benefits would you expect it to have for him?

xercise 4
Ethical issues in genetic choices

Susan has discovered that she is pregnant again. After several rough months, her doctor uses amniocentesis to check on the condition of the fetus. A genetic screening discovers that the infant has Down's syndrome (trisomony-21). The doctor recommends an abortion.

Write a brief paper explaining what do you think Susan should do.

Why might the doctor recommend the abortion?

What moral or ethical problem might arise?

Who should be able to determine whether or not an abortion is a good idea:

> Susan
>
> Her doctor
>
> Her family
>
> Society
>
> The government...?

This is a topic with many strong opinions and feelings associated with it. Be sure to discuss why you came to your conclusions and include any information or evidence that you have available that will support your position.

xercise 5

Critical periods for damaging effects during prenatal development

	Embryo									Fetus						Full Term			
	2	4	6	8	10	12	14	16	18	20	22	24	26	28	30	32	34	36	38
Nervous System																			
Ears																			
Eyes																			
Palate																			
Teeth																			
External Genitals																			
Heart																			
Upper Limbs																			
Lower Limbs																			

This figure indicates approximate time periods during prenatal development when damage from teratogens and other external influences can have the greatest effect. The first part of each darkened bar indicates the most sensitive period. The medium gray indicates a period of moderate sensitivity. The pale gray indicates a period of little sensitivity.

Answer the following questions using the figure above.

1. What part of the developing human being is most likely to be damaged during prenatal development?

2. If a mother has rubella during the 6th week of pregnancy, what kinds of problems might you expect to see in the infant?
   What if the illness is during the 20th week of pregnancy?

3. The drug thalidomide, a mild tranquilizer, was given to many pregnant women in the 1950's. Their infants were born with missing or undeveloped arms and legs.
   At what point during the pregnancy did the tranquilizer have this effect?

4. What parts of the premature infant are still sensitive to damage?

5. The heart begins beating when the infant is about three weeks old.
   Can the heart still be damaged at this point?

Exercise 6
Your Inheritance

We often speak of things that we have, or will, inherit from family members; Money from a parent, a painting from Grandfather, a dresser from an Aunt, clothing from an older sibling. Interview family members about things that are common in your family. Ask about common illnesses, occupations, appearance, or any other factors of interest to you.

Write a brief paper summarizing what you have learned about your inheritance. Try to categorize the observations into:

> things which are likely to be due to heredity
> things which are probably due to environmental influences
> and things which are due to a combination of both.

Exercise 7
Dominant and Recessive Genes and Phenotypes

When an infant is born it carries the combination of genetic material from both of its' parents. This genetic material can be seen in the appearance of the child, its' phenotype, or it may be carried invisibly in the child's DNA.

Imagine that you can create a child with the random combination of the following characteristics. (In reality, some of these genes are more or less prevalent in certain populations such as different ethnic groups. It is also possible for a person to be a Mosaic and have DNA for more than one combination.)

Flip a coin to determine the genetic contribution from each parent and enter it into the table. Then use colored markers or pencils to fill in the details on your "child."

Possible Traits

Head Dominant Trait	Tail Recessive Trait
Brown eyes	Gray, Green, blue, or hazel eyes
Curly hair	Straight hair
Dark hair	Light or blond hair
Non-red hair (blond. brunette)	Red hair
Normal skin coloring	Albinism (lack of pigment)
Thick lips	Thin lips
Roman nose	Straight nose
Earlobe free	Earlobe attached
Cheek dimples	No dimples

The Child's genotype

Contribution from Mother	Contribution from Father

CHAPTER 3
PHYSICAL DEVELOPMENT AND CHANGES

Many physical changes occur in an orderly fashion during development from infancy through late adulthood. Knowing the common pattern of growth changes before interpreting actual behaviors of health and illness can make interventions more appropriate and constructive. Growth is a continuous process (but not an even process) and it requires reliable evaluation over a period of time. Observation of a person's general appearance will allows a rough, yet important assessment of: nutritional status, posture, body movement, motor skills, coordination ability and speech development.

You may have questions regarding the implications of dynamic changes to the developing body and its parts. I hope that your questions will allow you to develop your own answers as you developing competencies you will need in your lifetime.

While this chapter will include statements that refer to the close relationship a body to cognitive, emotional and social learning in human development, the discussion will focus on physical development and change. Examples of two common physical problems can assist you in detecting evidence for these and other physical impairments that sometimes occur as a person ages.

Critical Issue – Physical Development: Child & Adolescent

In the first 18 months of life, an infant experiences many changes in physical growth. The head of a full term newborn is almost one-quarter the length of the body. In adulthood, the head is approximately one-eighth of the length of the body.

Other average newborn measurements include:

- head circumference of 32 to 38 centimeters;

- chest circumference of 12 to 13 inches;

- head to heel length of 19 to 21 inches;

- body weight of 6 to 9 pounds.

From this point on growth generally occurs gradually. The physical changes progress month to month and year to year until the healthy child is a fully functioning unit in late adolescence. The senses of vision, hearing, taste, and smell are present at birth and become more developed during infancy. Accurate measurements at birth are important as they provide a baseline for comparison of future growth.

The development of some parts of the body is slower than others.
For instance, during the first year of growth:

- Birth weight usually triples and the birth length will usually increase by 50%.

- Head size will increase by 33% whereas the heart size grows less rapidly.
  (These changes occur if the infant is free of disease and congenital disorders.)

Throughout infancy body organs enlarge and body systems become more mature and efficient. The average infant heart rate ranges 120 to 140 beats per minute. The heart rate becomes slower as the child grows older. The adult average heart rate is 80 to 100 beats per minute.

In the infant, the torso length is long in comparison to the limbs, whereas in adults it is just the opposite.

Body growth in infancy and adolescence is more rapid than at any other time of the life span. The growth in body length erupts in adolescent girls from age 10 to 12 years and in adolescent boys from age 12 to 14 years. The eventual adult height is approximately twice the height when 2 years of age.

The visual acuity of newborns is limited by their ability to change the focus of the lens. An indication of improving acuity and motor control is seen at 5 to 6 weeks when the infant can follow an object with his/her eyes. By three months of age, the ability to converge appears and the infant begins to reach for objects. Visual acuity continues to improve and 20/20 vision is reached at seven years of age.

Hearing is assessed in an infant by observing a startle or eye blinking in response to a loud sound. At approximately 4 months, the infant will turn his or her head towards the source of a sound. Speech development begins in the fourth month with babbling sounds. (Even a deaf infant will produce sounds at this age.) If the infant has adequate hearing acuity, the use of spoken words will begin between nine and 18 months of age. Most children develop intelligible speech by 6 years of age.

The normal newborn is toothless (edentulous). Most infants have teeth by 12 months and the complete set of 20 teeth has erupted by two and one-half years of age. The remaining teeth erupt by age 10 to 12 (with the exception of wisdom teeth).

Infant growth occurs rapidly and consequently, the caregivers must intervene to insure adequate physiological functions for survival. In the beginning of life, an infant is totally dependent on others. The need for nutrients, warmth, safety, sleep, and attachment require adult knowledge if normal physical, emotional, social, and cognitive growth of the infant is to be assured.

As the child matures, fine motor and gross motor coordination improves as neurons function more efficiently and muscles become developed.

During puberty, a normal deposit of subcutaneous fat occurs among females. This can have emotional and social as well as physiological effects as body image must change with a changing body. In females, the growth of pubic and axillary hair precedes menarche (which occurs from 11 to 16 years of age in the U.S.) by about two years. In the adolescent male, hair begins to appear on the face, chest, arms, legs, and underarms. The growth of pubic hair begins after the testes and penis begin enlarging.

This is a rapid period of growth. Nutrition is essential and adolescents require the caloric consumption of any age. Muscles increase in size and strength, and bones grow to their maximum length as the body readies for adulthood.

Adulthood

In young adults, few changes are seen, as the physical status of this period is essentially the same as late adolescence. At this time in life more physical changes are experienced in females due pregnancy. The next group of observable physical changes occurs in late adulthood.

In the period of growth and development up to late adulthood, normal changes are commonly viewed as positive and exciting. Many parents document the growth and compare the changes to charts of normative development to predict future growth. The following age related developments and changes are not generally treated with such enthusiasm. Predicting what occurs during this time span is not always reliable.

Heart muscle thickens with normal aging. In late adulthood, there are also changes in the blood vessels. One major change is loss of elasticity. This can result in increased resistance in the peripheral circulatory system causing a rise in blood pressure (hypertension). Contractions of the heart are less frequent and with less force. This affects the response to exercise; the person tires more easily than before.

In women, menstruation ceases (menopause) usually between the ages of 45 and 55 years of age. The ovaries decrease their production of estrogen. This decrease is related to hot flashes and the mood changes reported by some women. Reproduction for women after age range is rare. Between 40 and 55 the male testosterone production gradually declines. This does not have as dramatic an effect as menopause but eventually can prevent reproduction for men.

Thinning of hair is common. Hair may change to paler shades of the original color or white due to decreased pigmentation. Eyelids droop (loss of elasticity), eyes do not dark adapt as quickly, and peripheral vision is decreased. Even in people who have been nearsighted for a period of time may need eyeglasses for reading (Presbyopia).

Hearing loss is more noticeable after the age of 60. Presbycusis, the most common impairment, is the result of a decrease in ability to hear high-pitched sounds. (This problem affects more males than females.) Hearing loss results in reduced information from the environment and in social interactions and may result in social isolation. Thus emotional, social, and psychological ramifications could occur. The organs of balance in the inner ear may also be affected.

The normal physical changes in the elderly (sometimes called senescence) are usually structural and functional. There is a decrease in height due to the loss of collagen in the inter-vertebral discs. There is a decrease in vision (presbyopia), smell and taste, as well as decreased peristalsis, decreased muscle tone and reaction time, and delayed esophageal emptying. Taste decreases in the flavors of salt, sweet, sour, and bitter. There is a prevalence of dentures as decaying teeth or gum shrinkage occurs. A slight decline in short-term memory may occur as the nervous system reaches the elderly stage. The ability to recall past events, however, may be unimpaired.

②Critical Issue - Physical Impairment:

Dementia - Alzheimer's Type

It was once believed all elderly people suffered a loss of memory and thus experienced confusion resulting from atrophy of the aging brain. Dementia is not a normal state that happens to all elderly people. Dementia is recognizable by a decline in mental status, cognitive skills, and social functions. Alzheimer's Disease, one form of dementia, is related to a degeneration of neurons and their supporting cells. This destruction creates disorders in thinking (altered thought process), speaking (aphasia), moving (apraxia), and emotion. Symptoms appear slowly and without warning. The disease progresses to the point of a vegetative state when death is a welcomed outcome.

The progress of the disease differs from person to person. Therefore, the care of the Alzheimer's patient is determined by the individual progression of the disease. Assistance for both the patient and the caregiver essential in order to prevent "burn out." The caregiver needs to be reminded, "Its not the person causing the problems, its the disease process".

There are many roles involved in assisting the Alzheimer's patient and the caregiver.

- You may need to spend time letting the caregiver and patient talk about their anger and despair.

- The patient may have a memory disorder, but even the caregiver may not be mentally as competent as he or she might wish. The caregiver is under a great deal of stress and may not remember concepts or be consistently unprepared due to time spent trying to get the patient through daily activities or to respite care.

- Even as a clerk in a store you might need to be flexible to cope with the confused lady who cannot figure out the correct amount due for her purchases.

- As an employer you might anticipate a valued 30 year employee (the patient) to become less functional and in need of a reassignment or release from employment. If the caregiver is your employee, absenteeism might cause you to release her. You may not see the sleepless nights searching for a wandering spouse, or the stress of no one understanding her predicament. Remember that she is the wage earner and needs the insurance coverage.

Imagine the following scene. How would you react?

Dick's father is always complaining about the stove burners being left on; the constant questions such as "What am I supposed to do now?" the restless searching for hidden items; and the unkempt appearance of his once immaculate wife.

Dick's mother is 68 years old, she doesn't express emotions. Sometimes she refers to Dick as Bill (her brother). She pays no attention to the grandchildren when they visit.

The physical impairment of Alzheimer's affects an increasing number of people. As our aging population increases, so will this malady. When the diagnosis of Alzheimer's Disease is established, frustration occurs for everyone involved. There is no known cure and this non-reversible disease progresses unpredictable; sometime gradually, sometimes quickly.

Diabetes Mellitus:

Let's look at an example of someone with a physical impairment, and see how the problems that he has change throughout his life.

When Tommy (age 11) and his mother come to the school to register for classes, they make it a point to inform the school staff that Tommy has diabetes mellitus, a metabolic disease.

Tommy's pancreas is not producing enough insulin to support the metabolism of carbohydrates, fats, and proteins. Without the production of insulin, glucose is unable to enter the cells where it is used as fuel. This causes a condition called hyperglycemia (increased sugar in the blood). Tommy receives injected insulin every morning before school to help his cells make use of the food he eats. His medical condition is called *Insulin Dependent Diabetes Mellitus* (IDDM).

Tommy's mother informs the school about Tommy's special needs.

- Tommy needs to use his *Home Blood Glucose Monitor* (HGBM) while at school

- He needs snacks to prevent a dramatic decrease in blood glucose level.

- He will need to carry hard candy in his pocket to be used as a source of glucose during an insulin reaction (hypoglycemia).

- He must be responsible for reporting side effects, deciding when and what to eat, and other aspects of personal care.

- Because of Tommy's age, physical development, and activity, these responsibilities may be very difficult for him. Even a knowledgeable adult may find it hard to tell the difference between hypoglycemia (pale skin, sweating, shallow respiration, shaky feeling and dizziness, etc.) and normal over exertion in a typical eleven year old. It is of utmost importance for everyone involved in supervising Tommy to understand the disease and to encourage Tommy's participation in his care.

- Tommy (His friends call him "Tom") has graduated from high school, college, and he is now 32 years old. He has been employed as a news reporter for 10 years. He seems to have adequately adjusted to his diabetic disease process over the past 21 years. His physician has had him increase his insulin dosage over the past few years as his body has grown. Occasionally, Tom will have a hypoglycemic reaction when he delays eating for too long.

  Tom is married to Cathy. She understands the disease and encourages him to eat when he needs to and to control his insulin levels. They generally have a normal and happy life together.

At age 52 Tom begins to experience problems related to poor circulation caused by the disease. Tom's news reporting job requires him to be on his feet many hours at a time. The lack of circulation damages the tissue in his feet and the lesions become easily infected. His physician informed him his blood pressure is elevated and if not curtailed could result in a stroke. Tom continues to monitor his glucose by using his HGBM. He is beginning to experience vision problems from capillaries in his eyes hemorrhaging and he has trouble reading the monitor accurately.

The diabetes is causing neuropathy. This condition impairs the functions of the circulatory and nervous systems. A common effect of neuropathy is male impotence. This has effected his relationship with Cathy, but they are still very close. She has learned to cope with his increased need for assistance.

At age 72 Tom has frequent infections and his neuropathy is now causing early symptoms of dementia. Sometimes he does not remember whether he has eaten or taken his insulin. Due to these developments and coupled with the age-related physical changes Tom is depressed. Cathy, his wife, in addition to her own physical changes, is under a great deal of stress due to Tom's increasing disability. What was a minor problem in their early years together has become an increasing concern as they have gotten older.

Even a disease process develops. We have different reactions to the same situation at different times, and a problem is very different when an individual is old rather than young.

esearch Question

Chapter two discussed genes and the environment. Individuals researching developmental changes are interested in examining the relationship between culturally determined eating habits and obesity. Are there differing levels of obesity in different cultures? For example: Are there more obese individuals in the United States than there are in Japan?

According to recent research, up to 15% of U.S. youth are obese (Centers for Disease Control, 1994). Obesity rates appear to be quite high in most Western countries and lower, by comparison, in Eastern and Pacific Rim countries (Maffeis et al., 1993). What are the factors that influence these differences? They may include:

1. differing levels of exercise,

2. varying amounts of fat in the average diet

3. availability of high fat fast food, or

4. availability of sedentary activities.

Chapter 3 - Physical Development

onclusion:

Because the age-related physical changes can be in addition to physical impairments, determining the needs of individuals may necessitate thinking about their social, emotional, cognitive, and psychological reactions. Various professionals will need to be consulted and to interventions prepared. Knowing about the normal aging process can help you to identify abnormal changes.

aper Topics

- Describe the process individuals use to make decisions about the placement of a loved-one in an Alzheimer's unit?
- What is known about the causes of Alzheimer's? Does Alzheimer's appear to have a genetic component?
- Are there specific treatments that are normally recommended for Alzheimer's Disease? If so, what are they?
- How might losing a particular sense affect an individual? What issues would need to be considered in the adjustment process for this individual? Would it be more difficult to make the adjustment for one sense more than some others? Would the ability to adjust depend upon the period of lifespan the individual is in? Why or why not?
- Chose a physical problem. Describe the causes, symptoms, and treatments for the problem in the context of developmental change.

uggested Readings

Benelli, C., & Yongue, B. (1995). Supporting young children's motor skill development. *Childhood Education, 71*(4), 217-220.

Caulfield, R. (1996). Physical and cognitive development in the first two years. Early *Childhood Educational Journal, 23* (4), 239-242.

Forest, C. M., & Clemons, J. M. (1996). The elderly's need for physical activity. *JOPERD, 67*(4), 57-61.

Howe, F. C. (1993). The kindergartner (through the sixth grader). *Child Study Journal, 3*(4), 239-325.

Kelly, J. R. (1993*). Activity and aging.* San Francisco: Sage Publications.

Missiuna, C., & Pollock, N. (1991). Play deprivation in children with physical disabilities: The role of the occupational therapist in preventing secondary disability. *American Journal of Occupational Therapy, 45* (10), 882-888.

Petray, C., Freesemann, K., & Lavay, B. (1997). Understanding students with diabetes: Implications for the physical education profession. *JOPERD, 68*(1), 57-64.

Sherrill, C. (1993). *Adapted physical activity, recreation, and sport.* (4th ed.). Dubuque, IA: W. C. B. Brown & Benchmark.

**esources**

Alzheimer's Association
919 North Michigan Avenue, Suite 1000
Chicago, IL 60611-1676
(800) 272-3900
email: info@alz.org   www.alz.org

American Diabetes Association
1660 Duke Street
Alexandria, VA 22314

xercise 1
Preschool Play

During recess with your pre-school students you determine they need more physical activity than playing with a basketball.
Acknowledging their normal growth and development, what additional items would you purchase for these 4 to 5 year olds?

What equipment would be inappropriate to buy?

Why would this equipment be inappropriate to buy?

xercise 2
Sensory Decline with Increasing Age

Seventy-five year old Miss Hunt, is experiencing a hearing loss that is age related (physical). She has always enjoyed being physically active as this allows her to visit with her many friends.

- How might Miss Hunt be affected by these diminished sensory organs?

- Is it likely that most of her immediate friends will also be affected?

- What other sensory deficits might her friends be experiencing?

- What other problems might they experience due to the age related physical changes?

- How might you go about finding data to support your suppositions?

xercise 3
Living With Diabetes

You have been asked to consult with Tom's family regarding the many physical changes since his diagnosis of Diabetes Mellitus at age 11. Review the information about Tom on the previous pages.

- What changes are age related?

- You have been asked how to improve Tom's life (at age 72).

- Your response is _____

- Tom's response would be:_____

- Who should make the decision?_____

- The best thing for Tom is:_____

- The best thing to do for Tom is:_____

- Consult with 4 others in your class and document the group's responses.

Exercise 4
How Healthy Are You?

You are a 35 year old married male. You are 5'8" tall and weigh 180 pounds. You are a college graduate. Your employment entails traveling out of town during the weekdays. You believe you are knowledgeable about the physical factors that pertain to your age-related group.

What behaviors do your weekend friends observe that demonstrate your beliefs about health and wellness as a way to prevent physical disease or disorders?

Are these the same behaviors your friends would observe the five days you spend out of town? If so, why. If not so, why not?

Exercise 5
Obesity in Children

As a school social-worker you decide that the parents of two obese children (one from an Afro-American family and one from a Japanese family) need to be informed about and perhaps counseled regarding obesity in children. You have observed these 8-year-old children consuming large quantities of food from their lockers and grabbing food from trays of others in the lunchroom. Additionally, these children have a patterns of frequent illnesses and they refuse to participate in physical activities during gym. The classmates have been ridiculing these children by calling them "fatty," "blimp," and "pig."

- In light of the cultural influences that may be a part of the children's families, what do you need to consider before planning to meet with the parents of these obese children?

- What do you need to know about the physical development of these two boys?

- How might you intervene to reduce the ridicule by classmates?

- What might you expect from the classmates as a reaction to your interventions?

xercise 6
Changes as we grow old

There are a number of physical changes that commonly appear during the adult years. Different individuals experience these changes at different times, and react to them differently. Common changes include:

Graying hair

Wrinkling skin

Farsightedness (Presbyopia)

Weight gain

Weight loss

Hunchback (Osteoporosis)

Reduced mobility of joints (Arthritis)

Loss of teeth

Digestive problems

Menopause

Interview adults who have and have not experienced some of these changes.

How do they feel about the change?

Are they afraid of the changes that may take place? Are they angry? Confused?

Do they wish that they had done more to prevent the changes from occurring?

Do they see these changes as a sign of incapacity in old age or decline?

Do they feel different about the changes now that they have happened?

CHAPTER 4
COGNITIVE DEVELOPMENT

Cognition refers to mental processes by which we acquire knowledge of our world and includes all mental activity. Cognitive development covers all changes that happen in mental abilities as well as skills from birth to death. The infant has rudimentary capabilities to make sense of her world and as a child progresses to being able to manipulate symbols and react intelligently to the world. During adolescence, she becomes capable of abstract, hypothetical thought. As described in Chapter One, theories used to explain human behavior drive the researchers focus or perspective. Mechanistic theories dominated early research on cognition and energy was directed toward understanding learning and perception. Social learning theorists assumed importance in the second half of this century. Two important perspectives appear to dominate most accounts today, Piaget's structural-functional approach and information processing theory. Currently, researchers with an information-processing perspective dominate cognitive developmental research and seek to understand what happens between the stimulus and response. Organismic theorists, such as Piaget and Bruner, are concerned with the acquisition of concepts and ideas.

Critical Issue: The role of nature-nurture (heredity-environment) in development

Four decades ago Anastasi (1958) wrote a paper entitled, "Heredity, Environment and the Question How?" Her major point was that the historical "either/or" formulation with respect to heredity and environment, and the efforts to determine the proportional contribution of each, were the wrong issues to pursue. They were wrong because heredity and environmental factors interact with one another. She took the "interactionist's position."

Since Anastasi published her article, some of the same questions are still being asked. It is true that we have moved away from a simple "either/or" argument (which Anastasi indicated was already a dead issue in 1958), but the question of proportional contribution is still being debated.

According To Anastasi, the important question to ask is not "which" factor accounts for individual differences or "how much" each factor contributed, but rather "how" nature and nurture influence the development of the individual.

Critical Issue: The role of theory

Two types of theories, stage theory, and information processing have dominated the research in cognitive development. Piaget is the best known example of a comprehensive stage theory that emphasizes development from infancy to adolescence, of qualitative changes in knowledge structures. Information processing theories make the assumption that the mind is a system for storing and processing information which is processed in a series of stages that transform and manipulate the information. Jerome S. Bruner is a good example of this theoretical view. According to Bruner, during the sensorimotor period, the primary way infants represent the world internally is in terms of motor acts or the inactive mode. Children over two years of age use the iconic mode, which represents the world via mental images. School-age children are able to use language or the symbolic mode. Adults use all three modes situationally. Critics of information processing find this theory too narrow in its focus but its supporters point out that it has been helpful in stressing the importance of cognitive processes and structures.

③ Critical Issue: The nature and meaning of intelligence

As an individual grows from infancy through adulthood, it is necessary to react effectively to the many and constantly changing aspects of a person's environment in order to maintain life and to play an acceptable role in society. How well, how quickly, and how much a person will learn depends greatly upon his/her intelligence. As a matter of fact, intelligence is often conceived of as the ability to learn and profit from experience. It is basic to learning in school, vocational efficiency, avocations, and interpersonal relationships. A person's general intelligence is one limiting fact in life. Intellectual level influences the things of which we are potentially capable as well as those things of which we are not. For the developmentalist, the employer, the educator, the nurse, social worker, or for others who deal with people, the assessment of intelligence is one step in appraising an individual.

It is difficult to define intelligence. Attempts to define intelligence are in danger of giving it an existence that makes it real in such a way that it can be isolated and examined. A definition makes it easy to forget that "intelligence" is merely a word to indicate those behaviors, significant to human existence, which developmentalists and others have come to call intelligent.

④ Critical Issue: Measuring intelligence

"Intelligence," like "weather," is a word to describe phenomena in action. One does not measure intelligence as such any more than one measures the weather. In both cases, measurement is made of the behavior, not the concept. There is, however, one crucial difference between the concept intelligence and the concept weather. Many of the phenomena, which are grouped together and called weather, can be measures by more direct means than can the phenomena called intelligent behavior. In both cases, it is possible, however, after making measurements of the phenomena occurring, to return to the concept and to make a general judgment in its terms. One may call the weather good or bad, rainy or dry. One may say that a person's intelligence is high or low, and better in verbal or performance.

Intelligence has been defined by many prominent researchers. Several examples follow:

Spearman (1904, 1923): a general ability, which involves mainly the education of relations and correlates.

Binet and Simon (1905): the ability to judge well, to understand well, to reason well.

Terman (1916): the capacity to form concepts and to grasp their significance.

Wechsler (1930): the aggregate or global capacity of the individual to act purposefully, to think rationally, and to deal effectively with the environment.

Piaget (1972): a generic term to indicate the superior forms of organization or equilibrium of cognitive structuring used for adaptation to the physical and social environment.

Sternberg (1985, 1986): the mental capacity to automatize information processing and to emit contextually appropriate behavior in response to novelty.

Gardner (1986): the ability or skill to solve problems or to fashion products which are valued within one or more cultures.

Some definitions of intelligence imply that intelligence involves a single underlying component, while others stress intelligence as a number of distinctly separate abilities. Cattell and Horn have hypothesized that g and the primary mental abilities reflect two kinds of intelligence:
1 - fluid intelligence, which is not learned but based on biological maturation and functioning, and
2 - crystallized intelligence, which is based on learning and acquired knowledge, and thus has the potential to increase throughout the lifespan.

Guilford's "structure of the intellect" model has 120 primary mental abilities based on the interaction of three cognitive dimensions: content, operations, and products. These various definitions or approaches to intelligence have one problem, that is researchers/theorists use different measures and their findings are based on subjective evaluation. The most well known intelligence tests were developed by Binet and Simon and Wechsler. Wechsler's contribution was that he based IQ on a combination of verbal and performance measures. Perhaps the best model is one that posits a general intellectual factor and a small number of yet-to-be-determined specific abilities.

Research using major intelligence tests (both individual and group) has shown that intelligence tests are better used to a assess strong and weak points in individual thinking and interacting with the world than to rank individuals in terms of their general intellectual functioning. IQ tests are best used to predict school achievement, specifically school grades and future school performance.

5 Critical Issue: Is Intelligence Fixed or Changeable

If you were taking this course thirty years ago, you would have come away with the idea that your intelligence would peak during your college career and then begin a gradual decline for the rest of your life. Current thinking, however, suggests that much of intelligence remains stable through most of adulthood with some aspects actually increasing and a few showing a gradual decline. Secondly, you will hear that individual differences are the rule not the exception.

The reason of this dramatic change is that early analysis (60's and 70's) was based on cross-sectional studies (See Chapter 1). Recent studies are based on longitudinal research, which follow individuals over a period of time. Longitudinal studies have revealed that declines in intelligence may be attributed to illness and life situations rather than natural aging. For example, results of longitudinal studies confirm that elderly adults experience more decline in fluid than crystallized intelligence. The most consistent finding is that as people grow older, their rate of response slows which helps to explain behavioral changes seen in the elderly. When older adults are compensated for needing increased response time, their performance is often times equivalent to younger adults.

The classical patterns of intellectual functioning are based on typical reactions, but they are not universal. Patterns of aging and intelligence vary from person to person. Staying healthy and physically active counteract some of the effects of aging and the decline in intellectual functioning. Many scholars and artists produce their most important works at an advanced age.

An IQ score by itself is insufficient to use as confirmation of an individual's ability. While we have to assume that IQ tests are reliable and valid (See Chapter One), there are confounding variables that also contribute to actual performance. Environmental factors can contribute to an increase or decrease in intellectual functioning. Moreover, labeling children (or adults) solely on the basis of their IQ ignores the fact the IQ is only one piece of information that describes the complex and multiple nature of intellectual functioning.

esearch Question

Studies of cognition have expanded especially in the area of intelligence assessment. New markers of intelligence are being studied. Predictability of infant attention to novel stimuli, heart rate responses and brain wave patterns are contributing information about cognitive functioning during the performance of perceptual and cognitive tasks. These investigations may lead to improved predictability of adult intelligence in infants or to the possibility of cognitive dysfunction. In addition, definitions of intelligence are being expanded to include performance in areas beyond those of the traditional verbal and math abilities used to predict academic success and to suggest that this information can lead to modification of an individual's strengths and weaknesses in specific areas. What research can you find that examines these new areas of thinking? What effect would the findings have on decision-making by parents and school professionals?

Conclusions

Cognitive development is the study of knowledge structures and processes. Since those structures and processes can not be directly observed, they are inferred from the behavior of infants, children, and adults. Several methods, including observation, cross-sectional, longitudinal, experimental, and correlational are used to draw inferences and to test hypotheses and theories of cognitive development. Stage theory and information processing approaches are being reexamined in light of new findings that suggest intelligence is subject to situational and environmental factors. Traditional assessments of intelligence have recently been challenged by the concept of multiple intelligences.

aper Topics

1. Developmentalists still do not agree on whether we lose intellectual abilities as we grow older. A review of the literature will find three positions:
   yes, it does decline; no, it does not decline; and yes, it declines in some ways but not in others.

   - What position do you find is best supported in the literature?
     What experiences have you had that support your position?

2. Projects such as Head Start are based on the premise that intervention strategies can improve intellectual functioning in young children.
   How successful has Head Start been in providing disadvantaged children with skills and abilities that put them on an equal footing with middle class children by the first grade?
   Have the improvements continued beyond first grade?

3. Choose one of the following and review the literature to find out its importance for cognitive development:

   - Perceptual development;

   - Language

   - Motivation

uggested Readings

Armstrong, T. (1996). ADD: Does it really exist? *Phi Delta Kappan, 77*(6), 424-428.

Berk, Laura E. (1994). Vygotsky's theory: The importance of make-believe play. *Young Children, 50*(1). p. 30-39.

Bettelheim, B. (1987). The importance of play. *The Atlantic Monthly*. March issue. p. 35-46.

Bruner, J.S. (1966). *Toward a theory of instruction*. New York: W.W. Norton.

Bruner, J.S. (1973). *Beyond the information given: Studies in the psychology of knowing*. New York: W.W. Norton.

Eisner, E. W. (1997). Cognition and representation: A way to pursue the American dream? *Phi Delta Kappan, 78*(5), 348-353.

Gardner, H. (1983). *Frames of mind: The theory of multiple intelligences*. New York: Basic Books.

Piaget, J. (1926). *The language and thought of the child*. New York: Harcourt, Brace and World.

Piaget, J. (1952). *The origins of intelligence in children*. New York: International Universities Press.

Sternberg, R. J. (Ed.). (1985). *Human Abilities: An information-processing approach*. New York: W.H. Freeman and Company.

Thompson, A. M. (1996). Attention Deficit Hyperactivity Disorder: A parent's perspective. *Phi Delta Kappan, 77*(6), 433-436.

Vygotsky, L.S. (1962). *Thought and language*. Cambridge, MA: MIT Press.

xercise 1
Cognitive Development in Day Care

Form a group of students from your class. Try to find people who have different majors.
Design what you believe to be the ideal day care setting.
Place your emphasis on reinforcing cognitive growth.

Consider:

- Age of children
- Supervision
- Physical care
- Activities
- Toys

xercise 2
Transitions

Using the same group from exercise one, shift your planning and design the ideal adult day care program.
Place primary emphasis on cognitive functioning. (You may wish to discuss staff training as your emphasis.)

Consider

- Supervision
- Physical care
- Activities
- Cultural Differences

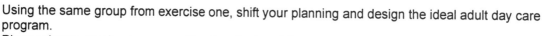

 **xercise 3**
Transitions

Using your readings here and your primary source text, outline the basic differences in cognitive development for primary, middle and high school students.
Also, suggest several teacher approaches for each based on the level of cognitive development.

- Primary/Elementary:

- Middle/Junior High:

- High School:

- College Student/Adult Learners:

 xercise 4
Transitions

Using our intergenerational family, assume that each one has suffered an illness that requires major intervention.
Choose an illness to discuss.
How would you design your intervention taking into account the cognitive level of each?

- Grandparent:

- Parent:

- Child

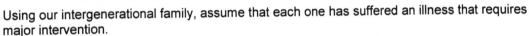

 xercise 5
Transitions

Many measures have been developed to test creativity. One approach has been to use remote associations. On the next page you will find a fifteen-item questionnaire similar to the one developed by Sarnoff Mednick (1963).

Give the questionnaire to a group of individuals (remember to get informed consent). Are there differences between male and female results?
Are there differences in results based on age?
Academic major?
What other comparisons can you think of?

Design a study. Think about the following:

What is an appropriate sample size?

What is your hypothesis or research question(s)?

What effect may the test or the design have on your conclusions? (Hint: reliability and validity)

Remote Associates Test

Directions: Find a word that the three given words have in common. For example:

paint	**doll**	**cat**

The answer is "house" –

"house paint,"	**"doll house,"**	**"house cat."**

1.	stool	powder	ball
2.	blue	cake	cottage
3.	man	wheel	high
4.	spelling	line	busy
5.	handle	hole	police
6.	wood	liquor	luck
7.	motion	poke	down
8.	knife	up	high
9.	plan	show	walker
10.	house	village	rope
11.	painting	bowl	nail
12.	made	cuff	left
13.	hop	side	pet
14.	bell	tender	iron
15.	bull	tired	hot

Answers				
1. foot	4. bee	7. slow	10. green	13. car
2. cheese	5. man	8. jack	11. finger	14. bar
3. chair	6. hard	9. floor	12. hand	15. dog

xercise 6
New Parents Workshop

Several community members have heard that you are currently taking a course in life span development. They have asked you to do a workshop for new parents on cognitive development.

> What would you choose to present?
> Prepare an outline for your presentation.
>
> Remember, you can not cover everything.
> What is most important to tell them?

xercise 7
Imaginary Audience

Young children often seem oblivious to what is occurring around them although when something that interests them is said, it turns out they have been listening after all. As teens, self-consciousness makes us so self-aware that we may actually misinterpret others' actions. For example, people laughing may be misinterpreted as laughing at us. Some adults retain this immature attitude while others seem to become less self-centered. All of these stages of development are important.

Consider the writing of David Elkind and his concept of the "imaginary audience." How might an imaginary audience be used by young children?
How does it help them gain self-confidence or learn to get along with others in later social situations?
Why, then, during adolescence might it become problematic, while in adulthood, people who "rehearse" things ahead of time are considered to be well functioning?

Try keeping a journal for a week.
How often during the week do you catch yourself talking to yourself, or imagining that someone is watching or listening to you?
Did you make a decision on what to wear or what to say based on perceived opinions of what others might think?
What does this tell you about your own level of cognitive development?
How does your level of cognitive functioning (and maturity) influence your behavior towards others?

xercise 8
Piaget's Theory of Cognitve Development

Piaget's theory of cognitive development predicts that the preoperational child will not be able to understand certain situations because of his or her inability to conserve. As adults most of the conservation tasks he used seem too easy, and it may be hard to understand how a child can insist that her brother got more juice when the only difference is in the shape of the glass.

Since we understand conservation, we often find it humorous when someone else does not. Find examples of cartoons or jokes that are based on an understanding of conservation. (The "Family Circle" cartoon often has very accurate portrayals of the conservation problems of toddlers.)

Attach the cartoon or write out a description of the joke.

Then tell why it represents the failure to conserve.

For example:

A woman walks into a bakery and buys a cake. The clerk offers to cut it and the woman says, "No thank you. I only want one piece. I am on a diet."

In this case the woman does not seem to understand that she will eat the same amount if she eats the whole cake, whether it is cut into pieces, or not.

(This tells us something about getting a child to eat an undesirable food. Don't cut it into small pieces. Then there is MORE of it.)

CHAPTER 5
SOCIAL DEVELOPMENT AND CHANGE

Without a doubt the social changes one confronts within the context of development can have a profound impact on who one becomes. It can certainly be said that "development does not occur in a vacuum". What this means is that development must be considered within the broader context of an individual's life. The purpose of this text is not to address how individuals are affected by social changes across the lifespan. Instead, this chapter will focus on major issues within a social context that have an impact upon an individual's development. In particular, the following issues will be addressed:

the effects of change on social development

the formation and importance of friendships, and

the ramifications of shyness and withdrawal.

Critical Issue - The Importance of Environments & Change in Social Development

Individuals and environments function in a reciprocal relationship. This means that individuals are affected by their environment and, at the same time, these individuals are having an effect on that environment. Environmental change (be it moving to a new school, the addition of a new family member, or getting a divorce) dictates change on the part of every individual whose life includes that aspect of the environment. Likewise, individual differences play a role in influencing the extent to which any given individual can respond appropriately to the necessary change. For example, an individual who is highly "flexible" may be better able to handle environmental change than someone who is more "rigid" or "set in his ways".

Successful social development requires a fine integration of the individual and the myriad of environments within which that individual must function. Some crucial issues to consider are: (1) what important environments affect social development and change, (2) what changes might occur within these environments, (3) what social changes will individuals confront, and (4) what factors influence the relative "success" or "failure" of the individual in adapting to these social changes.

Environments That May Initiate Self-Change

It has been said that *as environments change, people change*. Environments are powerful determinants of an individual's behavior. The whole concept of peer pressure revolves around the power of environments and the individuals within them. A child who has low self-esteem, for example, may be more likely to engage in peer pressure activities in an attempt to "fit in", be accepted, or be seen as just one of the group. One of the worst feelings for a child is to feel like she or he stands out. If blending in is the goal, then, the easiest way to accomplish that is by doing what everyone else is doing (e.g., Bronson, 1972; Covington, 1992; Osborne, 1996; Tomasello, 1993).

As environments change, it is expected that individuals will make adjustments to their own behaviors, efforts, etc. to compensate. What if the individual doubts that he or she can be successful in making such changes? Where does an individual turn for information in this case? It is quite likely that the individual will look to similar others, note how they are compensating, and model his or her own behavior accordingly (e.g., Festinger, 1954; Wheeler, 1991). This is not always a bad thing. Sometimes the individuals around us are better prepared to handle change or are simply more knowledgeable about what change is required. In these cases, comparing self to others and making adaptations is beneficial. Sometimes, however, the individuals around us are no better prepared to adjust to the environmental change than we are.

Critical Issue - Family

Family is clearly an important source of social relationships. Even adults who report not being particularly close to their siblings, for example, still report knowing they can count on those siblings in a time of need (Hale, 1998). Parenting choices also have a clear effect on children. Adult children who report having to "fend" for themselves in the family environment are significantly more likely to endorse the controversial idea of "licensing parents" (Keesling, 1998).

Research by Main, Kaplan, and Cassidy (1985) showed the long-term impact of parenting choices. These researchers showed a clear relationship between parents' internal models of attachment (their thoughts about their childhood experiences and current relationships with their parents) and the attachment bonds developed with their own children. In other words, individuals' parenting choices as adults are shown to be related to how they, themselves, were parented.

Osborne (1996) summarized decades of research on factors influencing self-concept and self-esteem development. Again, internal models are shown to be important. Modeling and patterns of reinforcement from parents have been shown to influence how children will interpret the positive and negative events in their lives. Children who are required to accept responsibility for all of their failures and be "humble" when succeeding, for example, are more likely to develop self-esteem problems than children who are taught to accurately assess their role in the positive and negative events in their lives. Presumably, the former children develop an internal model of self-assessment that suggests "if things go wrong, it's my fault but if things go right, somebody must have helped me."

Linehan (1993) suggested children who are raised in environments that are self-invalidating (the focus on the child's wants and experiences is minimized) are significantly more likely to develop Borderline Personality Disorder than children reared in self-validating environments.

Critical Issue - Friendship

We have looked at the relationship between environmental change and self-change. In addition, we have glimpsed some of the powerful effects of family on self-development. But self development does not just occur within the context of the family or the classroom. At the same time that the individual is trying to negotiate an identity, he or she is also developing and/or maintaining friendships. Would identity have an affect on and be affected by one's friendships? The answer would certainly seem to be "yes".

The development of friendships is influenced by different factors at different times in our lives. Several themes, however, underlie those friendships. A short list of those themes would include:

similarity - we tend to develop friendships with others who are similar to us in terms of age, gender, interests, race, values, etc.

proximity - we tend to develop friendships with others who live physically close to us.

benefits - we tend to form friendships with individuals who can have some positive benefit for us. If I want to become part of a certain group, for example, I may do that by becoming friends with a group member first.

Although the nature of these variables may change as we grow older (we tend to have a lower percentage of same-sex friends as adults than we did as adolescents, for example), the same basic factors influence friendship development and maintenance across the lifespan. There is an obvious connection between self-concept, self-esteem, and friendships. If we have low self-esteem, we are less likely to put our self into situations where friendships can be formed. This might cause us to feel isolated which, in turn may further feed our low self-esteem. Friendships are important for a variety of reasons including social support but the primary importance seems to come from the impact friendships have on our sense of self-worth (e.g., Osborne, 1996). If individuals like me, it confirms my feelings that I am "worthy".

 # Critical Issue – Shyness and Withdrawal

It makes sense that shyness and withdrawal will be related to one's social development. If I have low or uncertain self-esteem, I am unlikely to put myself into social situations because I doubt my ability to be socially successful. The fewer social situations I put myself in, the lower my social skills and another vicious cycle has started. Social skills deficits have been linked with a variety of childhood and adolescent problems including: depression, anxiety, and impulse control disorders (Frame, Matson, Sonis, Fialkov, & Kazdin, 1982).

One of the major problems with shyness and withdrawal is that these problems tend to perpetuate themselves. This means that shyness tends to initiate behaviors that reinforce that shyness. This cycle (as previously mentioned) can become a trap. The shy individual does not put himself or herself into social situations. Yet these very situations are necessary experiences if one is to develop adequate social skills. This lack of social skills training makes it likely that the individual will come across poorly if he or she does choose to engage in a social situation. The negative feedback received from a social "failure" further reconfirms in the individual's mind a fear of social situations. This, of course, leads to further withdrawal, magnifies the lack of social skills, and perpetuates the problem.

The educational setting is probably one of the best for attempting to turn this pattern around. It is also, however, one of the environments that is most likely to feed the problem. The question for the educator, then, is how to develop a classroom environment that supports the development of social skills without creating the potential for social "failure". This is one of the "critical thinking" questions included at the end of the chapter for student reflection.

Some individuals exhibit such extreme shyness and withdrawal as to be labeled "socially phobic" (Beidel, 1991). These individuals show biological reactions (e.g., increased pulse rate) to the mere thought of public performance. Again, the question becomes how to pull the withdrawn child into social interactions without running the risk of public humiliation or failure. In 1890, psychologist William James suggested that the single most effective method for enhancing self-confidence is task accomplishment. Educators, teachers, parents, and psychologists alike, then, must consider methods for engaging the child in successful social interactions where his or her skills are most likely to lead to social success.

esearch uestion

A social development related research question that has generated a lot of interest in the social psychology literature is, "does proximity (closeness to us in physical space) or similarity (closeness to us on issues, values, and activities that matter to us) most strongly affect liking and the development of friendships?". Initial research suggested that proximity was a powerful predictor of liking (e.g., Burr, 1973). Other research, however, clearly suggested that similarity was a primary predictor of liking (e.g., Byrne, 1971). So, how do we answer this question? As with most issues in psychology, it is really not the controversy it might at first appear to be. Newer lines of research confirm what you might already suspect - it is both. Certainly proximity influences the number of opportunities we have to get to know someone well enough to discover whether they are similar to us (Arkin & Burger, 1980).

This newer way of thinking about proximity has helped to resolve this research question. Rather than thinking of proximity as a matter of "geographic distance", the research by Arkin and Burger and others indicate that we should think in terms of "functional distance". Functional distance is defined as "the number of times that people's paths cross" (Myers, 1994). In this sense, the more times our paths cross with the same person, the greater the opportunity for us to have interactions that indicate our degree of similarity. From here, similarity plays a key role in determining how much you will "like" someone. In turn, the more we like someone, the more likely we are to describe her or him as a "friend".

onclusion:

Certainly this chapter does not touch on all of the aspects or implications of social development. Individuals in the helping professions need to be aware of the importance of social development and to understand the linkages between social development and behavior.

A core theme in this chapter has been one of "cycles".

We have all heard the tired cliché that "misery loves company". In essence, this tends to be true. The research literature on self-esteem, however, suggests that "misery loves miserable company" (e.g., Campbell & Lavallee, 1993; Osborne, 1996; Pelham, 1991, Tice, 1993). Individuals with low self-esteem, individuals who are shy, and individuals who are socially withdrawn, perpetuate that very misery because it is all they know. If we are to break that negative cycle of development, we must consider what roles we play in these processes within our given professions.

As educators, we need to consider what affect we have on the individual who is shy. If we ask such a student to step to the front of the class and read an essay, is this going to strengthen the negative cycle? What if the student comes to the front of the room, stutters horribly because of nervousness, and the rest of the students in the class laugh? Won't this student walk back to her or his seat even more certain that social situations should be feared? The methods we use within the classroom environment, the techniques we use for getting students involved in the discussion, the degree to which we allow students to work on their own or require public performance, all have an impact on the individual students and their self-related development.

Another fundamental theme within this chapter has been one of change.

Individuals in the helping professions must remember that change requires change. Changes in our environments dictate changes in our selves. But it is important to remember that environments include other people. As the individuals who are important to us undergo change, it forces us to change as well. If we are a sixteen year old who has always had mother at home to cook for us, clean our clothes, organize our schedules, and remind us to complete our projects, imagine the change that we will have to go through if mom decides to pursue a college education and announces, "I can't do all those things for you anymore". A key for the helping professional is to remember that change is not necessarily bad. The relative impact of change for the developing person is determined by how that change is handled and resolved.

A final theme that has permeated this chapter is one of crisis.

Erikson (1963) reminded us that crisis, in-and-of-itself, is not a bad thing. Individuals grow, mature, and develop as a result of the successful resolution of crises in their lives. In Erikson's writings, the term "crisis" primarily meant "challenge". To the extent that the individual confronts the challenge and can successfully resolve it, a stronger sense of self or identity will emerge.

Although crisis is inevitable, negative outcomes are not. Individuals in the helping professions must be prepared to help others confront their challenges, utilize their own strengths, and utilize challenges as important defining moments. The individual in the most serious self-related trouble is one who considers crisis to always be negative, doubts his or her ability to confront and/or resolve that crisis, does anything possible to avoid the crisis, and stagnates developmentally. Remember one of the primary themes of lifespan development outlined in the introduction to this text - growth is not possible without change.

aper opics

1. Consider the concept of "effort" in grade school. Read Martin Covington's book, Making the Grade published in 1992. Covington claims that many students do not try in school because effort without complete success is not rewarded. What things could be done in the school system to encourage youth to put forth effort, even if that effort is not completely successful? Interview at least three teachers and solicit their opinions on how to motivate youth to try harder in school and value academic success.

2. Lack of appropriate social skills has been clearly linked to low self-esteem and social development problems. Seek out information on what social skills are linked to self-esteem. What can be done to enhance and/or foster these social skills? Find and describe at least five variables discussed in the psychological literature as being important for the development of social skills.

uggested eadings

Barklay, R.A. (1995). *Taking Charge of ADHD: The Complete authoritative guide for parents.* New York: Guilford.

Baumeister, R.F. (1993). *Self-Esteem: The puzzle of low self-regard.* New York: Plenum.

Berk, Laura, E. (1994). Vygotsky's theory: The importance of make-believe play. *Young Children, 50* (1), 30-39.

Covington, M.V. (1992). *Making the grade: A self-worth perspective on motivation and school reform.* New York: Cambridge University Press.

Hale, C. (1998). The effect of sibling relationship and birth order on development. Paper presented at the Butler University Undergraduate Research Conference, Indianapolis, IN.

Hofstetter, C.R., Sallis, J.F., & Hovell, M.F. (1990). Some health dimensions of self-efficacy: Analysis and theoretical specificity. *Social Science and Medicine, 31* (9), 1051-1056.

Keesling, D. (1998). *Contemporary attitudes of licensing parents.* Paper presented at the Butler University Undergraduate Research Conference, Indianapolis, IN.

Linehan, M. M. (1993). *Cognitive behavioural treatment of borderline personality disorder.* New York: The Guilford Press.

Main, M., Kaplan, N., & Cassidy, J. (1985). Security in infancy, childhood,and adulthood: A move to the level of representation. In I. Bretherton& E. Waters (Eds.), Growing points of attachment theory and research. *Monographs of the Society for Research in Child Development, 50* (Serial No. 209), pp. 66-104.

McWhirter, J.J., McWhirter, B.T., McWhirter, A.M., & McWhirter, E.H. (1993). *At-risk Youth: A comprehensive response.* Pacific Grove, CA: Brooks/Cole Publishing.

Osborne, R.E. (1996). *Self: An eclectic approach.* Needham Heights, MA: Allyn & Bacon.

Shillingford, J.P., & Shillingford-Mackin, A. (1991). Enhancing self-esteem through wellness programs. *Elementary School Journal, 91* (5), 457-466.

Wittmer, D.S. & Honig, A. S. (1994). Encouraging positive social development in young children. *Young Children, 49* (5). p. 4-12.

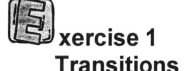xercise 1
Transitions

Let's take our intergenerational family as an example. Austin is 18 years old and has just moved to college. This transition will affect every member of the family in some way. The parents are faced with the reality that their "children" are becoming "adults"; Austin is trying on a new self-image called "college student", and the siblings remaining at home must negotiate what changes, if any, this transition will have on their position in the family.

Jessica, for example, might start wondering if Austin's choice to go to college will become an expectation of her. Jessica was described as upset because her parents are not reacting particularly well to her increased desire for independence. It is possible, of course, that Susan and Thomas (the parents) are trying to strengthen their "hold" on Jessica and Kyle because Austin has left the home. If the parents are experiencing any sort of identity crisis because of Austin leaving the home, it is likely to have an impact on their relationship with the remaining children.

Using information from this chapter and the appropriate chapter(s) from your main text, address the following issues:

Briefly discuss how Austin's moving away to college might cause self-related change for each of the other family members.

- What negative effects might there be?

- What positive effects might there be?

- Why does self-change on the part of one family member necessitate self-change in the remaining family members?

Exercise 2
Shyness and Withdrawal

Based on the discussions in this chapter and the readings from your primary course textbook, reflect on and provide answers to the following questions.

Imagine that you are a sixth grade teacher. One of your students seems painfully shy and is physically withdrawn. Discuss three things you might do within the classroom environment to help this child develop successful social skills. Keep the following issues in mind as you form your answers:

- How do you provide the student with social challenges but not run the risk of "making things worse"?
- How do you know that the method you are using matches the student's interests?
- What social skills is this individual lacking and how can you provide support in those areas?
- How do you accomplish this "drawing out" within the context of a diverse classroom with children of differing level of ability and different needs?
- Are there ways to get the parents involved in this process?

Exercise 2
Family Change

Susan Tran (from our intragenerational family) is thinking about going back to college to get her Master's Degree. She is thirty-eight years old, and has always done the majority of cooking, cleaning, shopping, and providing of transportation for the entire family even while teaching full-time. What advice would you give Susan about how to work with her husband and teenage children to accept her role as "college student". Keep the following themes in mind as you reflect and answer:

- when individuals close to us change, it requires change from us as well.
- crisis is bad only to the extent that we do not successfully confront and resolve that crisis.

xercise 4
Identity Change

You are a health care professional and you have a patient who has suffered major injuries from a car accident and is now blind.

This person tells you, "I have no reason to live. What good can I possibly be to my family without my eyes?".

Based on the discussions in this chapter, what might you say to this person and his family to help them better deal with this challenge in development?

As you consider your answers, keep the following thoughts in mind:

- Identity comes as much from what we cannot do as from the things we can do.

- Self-concept and self-esteem are linked, therefore, changes in our self-concept can have a profound impact on our feelings of self-worth.

xercise 5
A Sense of Self

How has this chapter helped you to understand the following phrase: "Self Perpetuates Self"?

How would you apply that phrase to your own life?

What are examples of times in which your own self-characteristics have caused problems for you?

What are examples of times in which your self-characteristics have helped you?

 **xercise 6**
"Teacher's Pet!"

Kyle Tran (again from our intragenerational family) has always enjoyed school, had a close group of friends, but was shy around most all other children. Now, due to school rezoning, Kyle has to go to a new school. Kyle is earning good grades, so the teacher goes out of his way to acknowledge his accomplishments.

Rather than being proud of their new classmate for his intellectual recognition, however, the other students tease Kyle about being "teacher's pet".

Using information from this chapter and the appropriate chapter(s) from your main text, address the following issues:

- How can Kyle make new friends at this new school given that his shyness will make it difficult for him to approach others?

- Kyle is confronted with a dilemma. He can continue to illustrate his intellect that garnered respect and recognition from the teacher or he can try to gain the recognition of his peers. What advice would you give to him and why?

- What impact might Kyle's recent diagnosis with A.D.D. have on his ability to make friends and continue to do well in school?

 **xercise 7**
Crises

Imagine a parent who is suddenly faced with the realization that all of the children have grown up and moved away. This adult may be wondering, "where do I go from here?". Individuals confront such "Identity Crises" many times throughout life. But "crisis" here is a relative term. Crisis is problematic only to the extent that we do not successfully resolve the crisis and have a stronger sense of self as the outcome of that resolution. Using information from this chapter and the appropriate chapter(s) from your main text, address the following issues:

- What factors might influence the degree to which this parent will experience a "crisis" as a result of this role change?

- How can the negative impact of such a role change be minimized?

xercise 8
Attention Deficit Disorder

In the description of our intergenerational family, the reader was informed that Kyle Tran has recently been diagnosed with Attention Deficit Disorder (ADD). The family must deal with the basic reality that one of the members has a "disorder", there will be a time period of psychological adjustment to this reality, and there will be some negotiating on the part of the family on how best to "deal" with this reality. With this particular type of disorder, it is important for the family to understand medically what is happening as well as considering the psychological and educational ramifications.

Using information from this chapter, additional resources, and the appropriate chapter(s) from your main text, address the following issues:

- What type of school difficulties might be related to this disorder?

- What impact(s) might this diagnosis have on Kyle's views of himself?

- What is known biologically about the cause(s) of ADD?

- Why are stimulants like Ritalin sometimes effective in treating ADD?

CHAPTER 6
EMOTIONAL DEVELOPMENT AND CHANGE

Without a doubt the social changes one confronts within the context of development One of the major themes discussed in the introduction to this text stated that, "It is the intermeshing of physical, cognitive, personal, and social development that gives each period of the lifespan, and each individual, a distinctive and coherent quality". As individuals develop and change in one aspect of their lives (such as physical change), it necessitates change in other aspects of life (such as emotional changes). The developing adolescent, for example, certainly will have emotional reactions to the physical changes occurring in her body. As the mirror reflects the individual's rapid march toward adulthood, he or she must confront, resolve, and integrate the associated emotions into the changing identity.

This chapter takes a brief look at emotional changes and the impact such changes can have on the developing person. After looking at emotional changes in a general sense, we will examine some of the implications of emotions and the effect such emotions have on the developing individual. Again, we will consider the issue of emotional change as thematic. Regardless of the phase of lifespan the individual is in, there are certain aspects of emotional change that will underlay each of those phases. As we progress throughout the chapter, we will consider the following critical issues:

- **What are emotions?**
- **What kind of emotional changes do individuals experience as they develop?**
- **What impact does emotional change have on other aspects of developmental change?**
- **How do emotions influence thinking?**

 # Critical Issue - What Are Emotions?

The literature on emotions suggests that emotions involve three components (e.g., Izard, 1992; Zajonc & McIntosh, 1992):

1. Physiological changes in the body (such as shifts in heartrate, increase in blood pressure, etc.).
2. Subjective or internal cognitive states (or how the individual interprets the physiological changes, prior experience with certain emotions, etc.).
3. Expressive behaviors (how those emotions are manifested in outward behavior such as facial expressions, bodily gestures, etc.).

One major difficulty in studying emotions comes directly from this listing of the components of emotions. Although recent evidence suggests that different emotions may involve activation of different areas of the brain, (e.g., Davidson, 1992; Davidson & Fox, 1988; Henriques & Davidson, 1991; Robinson, Kubos, Starr, Rao & Price, 1984; Tomarken, Davidson, & Henriques, 1990) the physiological reactions within the bodies of individuals may be quite similar. There seems to be no doubt, however, that the thoughts about and ability to regulate emotions may differ greatly from person to person.

Think about two individuals watching a violent movie. Perhaps one of the individuals "enjoys" such movies and the other does not. Both of these persons may experience physiological arousal in response to the film but the outcome of such bodily reactions could be quite different. The person who likes such movies may experience the arousal as indicative of a pleasant emotion while the other may experience the arousal as an unpleasant emotion.

Babies very quickly come to recognize various facial expressions and seem to understand the emotions that accompany tones of voice (Walker-Andrews & Lennon, 1991). It makes sense that this progression in discriminating and understanding emotions coincides with advances the infant is making in self-understanding. Both progression in responding to emotional cues and recognition of self in the mirror, for example, occur around 10 months of age.

 # Critical Issue - - What Kind of Emotional Changes Do Individuals Experience As They Develop?

The primary emotional change that individuals will experience as they develop is an increasing ability to regulate those emotions (e.g., Altshuler & Ruble, 1989; Izard, 1992; Sroufe & Waters, 1976). Very young children may have very little "self-control" over their emotions, whereas we would expect adults to have sophisticated control over them. Where does this self-regulation come from?

Surely, some aspect of emotional regulation is learned (Otaki, Durrett, Richards, Nyquist, & Pennebaker, 1986). Individual differences in emotional reactions, however, have also been shown to exist even as early as birth (Kagan & Snidman, 1991; Ruff, Lawson, Parrinello, & Weissberg, 1990; Thomas & Chess, 1977). Both learned and biological factors, then, seem to be involved in emotional expression and development.

The research indicates that children who develop secure attachments to their parents also are more secure in terms of self-confidence and social competence (Sroufe, 1989). Parenting choices, then, have been shown to strongly influence the degree to which children develop secure attachment. In particular, parents who accept the child and provide "contingent responsiveness" (defined as caregiving that is responsive to cues from the child and designed to fulfill the child's needs) seem to have children who are securely attached (Benn, 1986; Isabella, Belsky & von Eye, 1989; Sroufe & Fleeson, 1986). It is suspected that children reared in this fashion develop internal models of themselves as competent and valued. These internal models, then, have been shown to influence the manner in which these children will parent when they have children of their own (Main, Kaplan & Cassidy, 1985).

You may be confronted by children who are afraid and insecure. The manner in which you respond to this fear can affect the type of relationship you will have with that child. In addition, the child's self-related feelings will influence his or her behaviors within the educational setting. Children who are insecure, for example, have been shown to engage in behaviors in the classroom that result in negative outcomes, thereby reconfirming their negative self-expectations (e.g., Covington, 1992, Goode & Watson, 1992; Osborne, 1996).

Children who are insecure or uncertain about themselves may be likely to experience the kind of self-regulation of emotional difficulties mentioned previously. To the extent that such inability to regulate emotions result in punishment within the school setting, the negative cycle can perpetuate itself. Students may act out in the classroom less out of a desire to be disruptive and more out of a desire to self-protect (e.g., Covington, 1992). Hospitalized children also feel this loss of control.

In this fashion, the person who is aware of the linkage between emotional development and behavior will be in a much better position to respond to these issues when they arise.

Critical Issue - What Impact Does Emotional Change Have on Other Aspects of Developmental Change?

Emotional development can have a profound affect on the individual's developing sense of self (e.g., Freud, 1905; Lewis, 1990, 1991; Lewis & Brooks-Gunn, 1979; Piaget & Inhelder, 1969). It is easy to imagine how emotional and self-related changes can become intertwined, and under negative circumstances become problematic.

Researcher Diana Baumrind (1971) discovered a direct relationship between the parenting style of parents and the emotional development of their children. From her research, three parenting patterns emerged. **Authoritarian** parents are punitive, strict and lack sympathy for the child. They interact with the child in a manner that clearly signals that the parent's will is most important and the parent does not negotiate with the child.

Permissive parents, on the other hand, do not provide discipline. These parents allow the child complete freedom and seem either detached or so concerned about being their child's friend that they do not want to jeopardize that by providing limits.

In the middle between these two styles, then, are **Authoritative** parents. These parents provide discipline and guidelines but allow the child feedback in the relationship and also allow the child choices. The relationship between the parent and child in this latter case is one of mutual respect and a give and take.

It is not surprising that the style of parenting utilized is directly linked to emotional development and emotional maturity in the child. Children raised by Authoritarian parents seem to be emotionally withdrawn, lack trust, and are unfriendly. Permissive parenting results in children who are immature and unhappy. These children were more likely to throw tantrums and have greater problems in controlling their feelings when things did not go their way. Lastly, Authoritative parenting results in children who are happier, more independent, friendlier, and more cooperative. These children seem to trust the world and believe that they can take an active part in that world.

Social skills have been directly linked to self-esteem and situational success (e.g., Braza, Braza, Carreras & Munoz, 1993) and lack of social skills in childhood has been implicated in the development of emotional disorders in adolescence (Asendorpf, 1992). From this literature, it seems quite important to address the linkage between self-related development and emotional development. Individuals who feel competent approach situations with entirely different motives and are better prepared to emotionally adjust to whatever might happen within that situation (e.g., Osborne, 1996).

In addition to the immediate problems that lack of emotional flexibility can cause, research also suggests that individuals who feel emotionally incompetent in social situations engage in behaviors that perpetuate the problem (e.g., Langston & Cantor, 1989; Osborne, 1996). In this pattern, the individual lacking in social skills is painfully aware of the deficit. Because of this awareness, he or she assumes the worst is going to happen in a social situation. Due to this pattern of self-defeating cognitions, then, he or she will either choose to avoid the situation or act very guarded and unresponsive if the situation is unavoidable. In either case, the result is the same. The person does little to successfully build the social skills that are so sorely needed.

The individual who is experiencing challenges in emotional development surely is experiencing problems in other areas as well. Any efforts to help this individual get his or her emotional development back on track must take multiple paths as well. A teacher will need to find ways to address both the emotional regulation and shyness problems if he or she is truly going to help the student make developmental progress. It would also be wise to create educational strategies that center on theme number ten from the introduction which states, "we are active in our own development".

Very little can be done about the student's shyness, for example, just by calling on him in class. Instead, it might be better to find ways that the student can "plug" into the class based on his interests. In this fashion, he will be contributing to the class (and developing those very important social skills already discussed) because he wants to and not because he is being forced. Any social successes that he has of his own volition, then, can be credited to his self.

 # Critical Issue – How Do Emotions Influence Thinking?

Current moods have been shown to influence how individuals process information (e.g., Isen, 1987). Individuals who are in a good mood tend to interpret ambiguous information more positively than individuals who are in a bad mood (Fiske & Neuberg, 1990). Baron (1993) showed that individuals who have received favorable feedback rate job applicants with ambiguous qualifications more favorably than others who were given unfavorable feedback. If emotions influence the manner in which information is processed, it also stands to reason that emotions would influence memory as well.

Forgas (1991) and others have shown that information that is consistent with our mood is easier to remember than information that is incongruent with our mood. In addition, Isen and Daubman (1984) showed that mood influences the manner in which information is organized in memory. Individuals who are in a positive mood were shown to include a wider range of information in their memories.

Moods (as associated with attitudes) were shown by Fazio, Sanbonmatsu, Powell, and Kardes (1986) to influence the speed with which individuals could recognize presumably unrelated information. Results from this study showed that subjects were able to recognize hidden words significantly faster when they were consistent with their attitude (as activated by a stimulus word presented on the computer screen) than when it was inconsistent with their attitude. For example, subjects showed a word they disliked, like "liver, recognized negative hidden words (such as "awful" or "disgusting") significantly faster than positive hidden words (such as "wonderful" or "pleasant").

Research suggests that moods affect susceptibility to persuasion (e.g., Mackie & Worth, 1989) and the likelihood of making risky decisions (e.g., Arkes, Herren, & Isen, 1988). Individuals who are in a good mood, for example, are more likely to make risky decisions when the potential losses are minimal and are significantly less likely to make risky decisions when the potential losses are significant. Individuals who are in a good mood may also be more vulnerable to persuasive messages. Individuals in a bad mood seem more motivated to scrutinize the persuasive message which results in less effective persuasion (e.g., Smith & Shaffer, 1991).

 # esearch uestion

Emotions are the same the world over. Right? This question has been a very important one in research on emotions. Significant research has been devoted to assessing similarities of emotions and emotional expressions across cultures. The name most often associated with such research is Paul Ekman (Ekman & Friesen, 1971). In this groundbreaking research, stories were told in the native language of the subject being studied. After the story, photographs of faces displaying three different emotions were presented and the subject was asked to pick the photograph that matched the emotion expressed in the story. There was remarkable agreement regardless of the culture or the language.

But is this data enough to convince us that there are no cultural differences in emotion? Certainly not. If we engage in just a bit more thought, we are likely to decide that display of emotions is not equivalent to the experience or the expression of that emotion. Again, Ekman and his colleagues (e.g., Ekman, Friesent, & Ellsworth, 1972) engaged in research on this issue. These researchers found that although cultures are fairly consistent with how certain emotions are expressed in terms of facial gestures, these same cultures can also differ quite dramatically on the "display rules" associated with emotions. Display rules are "norms about when certain emotions should or should not be expressed or norms about when to express emotions that we might not actually be feeling." If someone tells us that it is "wrong to laugh at a funeral", this is an emotional display rule. These rules vary widely from culture to culture and even with subcultures within the same country.

Why is knowledge of display rules important? Although there can be many reasons, one of the most important, perhaps, is so that we do not violate those rules within another culture. One of the authors of this text clearly remembers attending a football game at The University of Texas at Austin during graduate school. The team is nicknamed "the Longhorns" and it is common to see fans making a longhorn type symbol with their hands and gesturing toward the football field. On this particular Saturday, one of the psychology faculty had brought several visiting dignitaries from another country to the game. When the longhorns scored and the fans gesticulated, the dignitaries were livid. It seems that in their culture such an emotional display is reserved for those times when you want to publicly make a very nasty statement (that we will not translate for you!) about one's mother. It took a lot of explaining and an interpreter to avoid an international incident! Just one more reason that an awareness of culture and doing research about other cultures is so important.

onclusion:

The preceding discussions clearly suggest that emotional development is linked with development in other areas. Individuals who have problems with emotional development are likely to have problems with self-development as well. Children raised by Authoritarian parents, for example, do not seem to develop the self-confidence and independence than children raised by Authoritative parents have. Certainly, such differences will have an impact on the development of friendships, peer relationships, or even intimate partnerships. Educators, psychologists, and health care professionals will all be confronted by situations in which emotional development becomes an issue. The degree to which the helping professional can respond to these situations is linked to the degree of his or her understanding of emotional development.

Teachers looking out across a classroom surely understand that the students differ as much emotionally as they might intellectually. Many classrooms are designed to accommodate the many intellectual needs of the students but how many are designed to address the child's emotional needs? Moods have been shown to affect information processing, social development, and social skills. Individuals who are lacking in emotional development are at risk for self-esteem problems and may have problems developing desired relationships with others. Helping professionals can aid these individuals by providing guidance and support in the following areas:

1. Effective coping with emotional crises,

2. Learning to deal more effectively with peers,

3. Discovering the impact that emotional development has on information processing and academic performance,

4. Developing an understanding of the emotions and the emotional needs of others, and

5. Developing the social skills that will help those individuals be more aware of and responsive to the perspective of others.

Paper Topics

1) How do attachment patterns that develop during childhood relate to development during adolescence? Discuss at least four aspects of adolescent and adult development that could be influenced by attachment during childhood (forming a significant love relationship, for example).
Describe the four major parenting patterns and list at least three characteristics of children reared with each pattern.
What long-term effects might these styles have on people?

2) List four emotions and consider the impact these emotions can have on thinking. What is the relationship between emotion and memory?
If you wanted to enhance a person's memory, how could you utilize information about emotions to do this?

3) If different emotions only create slightly different physiological reactions in the body, how could you explain the fact that emotions "feel" so different?
What role might culture play in the expression of emotions?

Suggested Readings

B Asendorpf, J.B. (1992). A Brunswikean approach to trait continuity: Application to shyness. *Journal of Personality, 60*, 55-77.

Berglas, S. (1986*). The success syndrome: Hitting bottom when you reach the top.* New York: Plenum Press.

Covington, M.V. (1992). *Making the grade: A self-worth perspective on motivation and school reform.* New York: Cambridge University Press.

Crockenberg, S.B. (1986). Are temperamental differences in babies associated with predictable differences in care-giving? *New Directions for Child Development, 31*, 53-74.

Goode, C.B., & Watson, J.L. (1992*). The mind fitness program for esteem and excellence.* Tucson, AZ: Zephyr Press.

Izard, C. (1992). Basic emotions, relations among emotions, and emotion-cognition relations. *Psychological Review, 99*, 561-565.

Langston, C.A., & Cantor, N. (1989). Social anxiety and social constraint: When making friends is hard. *Journal of Personality and SocialPsychology, 56*, 649-661.

Main, M., Kaplan, N., & Cassidy, J. (1985). Security in infancy, childhood,and adulthood: A move to the level of representation. In I. Bretherton& E. Waters (Eds.), *Growing points of attachment theory and research. Monographs of the Society for Research in Child Development, 50* (Serial No. 209, pp. 66-104).

Osborne, R.E. (1996). *Self: An eclectic approach.* Needham Heights, MA: Allyn & Bacon.

Sroufe, L.A. (1989). Pathways to adaptation and maladaptation: Psychopathology as developmental deviation. In D. Cicchetti, (Ed.),*The Emergence of a Discipline: Rochester Symposium on Developmental Psychopathology (Vol. 1),* 13-40. Hillsdale, NJ: Erlbaum.

Yarcheski, A., Mahon, N. E., & Scoloveno, M. A. (1990). Stressors and ways of coping in mid-adolescent girls. *Canadian Journal Of Health Care Profession Research, 22*, 67-78.

xercise 1
Transitions and Parenting

Let us visit our intergenerational family once again. Austin, age 18 is moving to college. Certainly, this will be an emotional time for the entire family. Consider the emotions that the family may experience as they adjust to this event and develop answers to the following questions:

What emotions might the parents experience?
How can they make the smoothest adjustment?

How would the emotions and the adjustment differ based on the typeof attachment bonds Austin and the parents have developed?

If Austin and the parents have an Authoritarian relationship, what emotional adjustment issues might there be?

If Austin and the parents have a Permissive relationship what kinds of adjustment issues and/or problems might you anticipate?

If Austin and the parents have Authoritative relationship, what might you expect in terms of how all three adjust to Austin's move?

xercise 2
The Moody Student

Imagine that you teach 4th grade. One of your students comes in each day distraught and moody.

What potential impact could these feelings have on this student's performance in your class?

What things might you be able to do within the context of the classroom, to minimize the impact of these emotions on the student's performance?

Address the following questions as you generate your response:

- What aspects of the classroom environment itself may be generating these emotions for the student?

- What discussions might you have with the student to decide on what changes (if any) need to be made in the classroom?

- What role might social skills play in this student's expectations about the classroom environment?

- If poor social skills is a problem, what changes might we expect in academic performance if this student's social skills are enhanced? Why?

- What factors at home might be contributing to this student's emotional level?

 xercise 3

Recovering

You are a health care professional working in a community hospital. Based on the material covered in this chapter and your primary course textbook, discuss how emotions might influence the physical recovery of a patient.

Address the following questions as you put together your response:

1) What role might negative emotions play in physical recovery?

2) What role might positive emotions play in physical recovery?

3) What could you do as a health care professional to help patients develop a more positive emotional outlook about their physical condition?

4) What connections are there between the individual's identity (as in the previous chapter) and his or her emotional response to a physical condition?

 xercise 4

Moods and Memory

From a psychological perspective, discuss the importance of the following statement:

"moods influence what we remember and how well we remember it".

 xercise 5
"I'll Cry if I Want To!"

You are a teacher working with a sixth grader who you think is having difficulty regulating his emotions. In addition, you have noticed that this child is extremely shy and withdrawn.

Could these two characteristics be related?

Utilizing information from this chapter and the appropriate chapter(s) of your main text, discuss the following themes as they relate to how you would work with this particular child:

1) Development proceeds in multiple directions, entailing at times gains, at other times loss, and at still other times just change

2) Early experiences influence but do not determine later outcomes

3) Development has multiple causes.

 xercise 6
The Components of Emotions

Jerome is exhibiting "inappropriate" emotional reactions to events in his life. He laughs, for example, when other persons get hurt.

From a psychological perspective, discuss how each of the aspects of emotions could be influencing Jerome's emotional reactions.

These three aspects are:

<u>Physiological changes in the body</u> (such as shifts in heartrate, increase in blood pressure, etc.).

<u>Subjective or internal cognitive states</u> (or how the individual interpretsthe physiological changes, prior experience with certain emotions, etc.).

<u>Expressive behaviors</u> (how those emotions are manifested in outward behavior such as facial expressions, bodily gestures, etc.).

Exercise 7
Would You Tell Her She is Dying?

You have been told by a physician that a patient of yours is dying. Now you are working with that patient and this person asks you if he/she is dying.

How would you answer the following questions:

1) Would you tell him or her the truth? Why or why not?

2) What role(s) would the concept of emotional development play in your decision about whether to tell the person the truth?

3) Would your answer to the first question differ if it was a child? Why or why not?

4) Would your answer to the first question differ if it was a teenager? Why or why not?

5) Would your answer to the first question differ if it was a young adult? Why or why not?

6) Would your answer to the first question differ if it was an older adult? Why or why not?

7) Would your answer to the first question differ if the person asking was a girl (woman)? Why or why not?

8) Would your answer to the first question differ if the person asking was a boy (man)? Why or why not?

Exercise 8
Self Regulation

Choose some aspect of yourself (e.g., an emotion, your temper, your lust for chocolate) that you would like to do a better job of regulating.

Develop a plan for self-regulating the aspect you have chosen. As you develop this plan, answer the following questions:

1) Why have you chosen to regulate this particular aspect of yourself?

2) Will it be difficult or easy to regulate? Why?

3) What will the three biggest obstacles be to self-regulating this self-aspect?

4) How can you minimize the impact of each of the obstacles listed in #3?

5) Briefly describe your plan.

6) After one week - describe your progress.

Exercise 9
Defining a Friend

In this chapter the concept of friendship was discussed as it relates to emotional development. It is possible that the concept of friendship differs with age. If this is the case, then we might also expect that how a person defines "friend" would influence that person's emotional well-being.

Locate an individual from each of the following groups and ask those persons to define "friend" for you:

- a young child (age 6 or younger)
- a teenager
- a young adult (between the ages of 25 to 35)
- an older adult (age 55 or over)

After each of these persons has defined "friend" for you, ask each person the following questions:

How many friends do you think you have?
- young child
- teenager
- young adult
- older adult

How many of your friends are boys (men)?
- young child
- teenager
- young adult
- older adult

How many of your friends are girls (women)?
- young child
- teenager
- young adult
- older adult

Can an animal be a friend? If so, how?
- young child
- teenager
- young adult
- older adult

What is the difference between a "friend" and a "close friend"?
- young child
- teenager
- young adult
- older adult

What do the answers given for these questions suggest to you about the roles that friends play as individuals age?

CHAPTER 7
MORAL DEVELOPMENT AND CHANGE

Critical Issue - The relationship between cognitive and moral development

What is the parallel between cognitive and moral development? The goal of moral training is to produce a person who will direct his or her behaviors toward the good and away from the bad without continual external reminders (Freiberg, 1983). Freud believed that people were "good" either because they were afraid of not being liked or because they were afraid of being punished. Social-learning theorists today believe that moral and ethical behavior is more complex and related to a person's ability to reason (e.g., Kohlberg, 1975).

Children may learn their belief system from observing influential adults, from watching television, or from their peers. Young children are not bothered by questions of differing perspectives because they are not yet able to put themselves in another's place. They rely on the adults in their lives to make authoritative decisions about what is right and what is wrong. Even as they begin to accept that behavior is on a continuum (some offenses more serious than others; some acts of goodness less self-serving), their judgments continue to be egocentric and unalterable because of their cognitive level of reasoning. Eventually, as children begin to see other's points of view and to realize how different motivations underlie different actions, justice becomes an issue of social context and in terms of equity and equality (Freiberg, 1983).

Kohlberg believed that Piaget placed too much emphasis on the child's respect for rules and authority. He felt that young children's obedience was instead a recognition that adults are more powerful (Freiberg, 1983). What does this suggest to you about trying to instill in young children a sense of self-discipline? Is it possible? When considering the work of Kohlberg and Piaget, it is important to remember that people's experiences and beliefs color their views of human nature. For example, it is possible for two people of the same age to view "fairness" differently. Perhaps one person has been treated reasonably fairly during his or her lifetime but another feels he or she has not. It is likely that there will be consequences for the behaviors of these individuals based on their beliefs about the application of fairness.

Some interesting questions to consider in contemplating the link between cognitive and moral development include:

- Do you know any adults that seem not be able to move beyond Kohlberg's stage of conventional morality ?

- Do you know any adults who react as though they fit more with Erikson's description of "inferiority" rather than "industry?"

- Do you know adults who do not want to get involved in controversy or in situations that cause them to support their beliefs with action?

- If people move through stages of moral development as they do cognitive development, why does there seem to be more variance in the way adults behave than in the ways they are able to reason?

②Critical Issue - Does moral reasoning depend on culture or gender?

Is the stage theory of moral development valid and what happens when we apply it to different cultures or consider issues of gender? Research supports that the sequence of moral development is consistent (and continuous) regardless of ethnic or cultural context (Nisan & Kohlberg, 1982; Colby et. al., 1983; Snarey, Reimer & Kohlberg, 1985). At the same time, behavior is strongly influenced by the adults and later the peers with whom one associates. Expectations placed on persons by both culture and gender may influence moral behaviors. It has been said, for example, that the United States operates according to an "individualistic culture" (e.g., Hofstede, 1980). Phrases such as "looking out for number one", or "career ladder" reinforce this concept. There are other cultures, however, that are more "collectivist" in orientation (Hofstede, 1980). Within these cultures what one does either shines well on or can shame the entire family. Clearly, such an emphasis will result in differing patterns of moral behavior.

Carol Gilligan (1982; 1987) found compelling evidence to suggest that another element of moral reasoning exists, that of care. Research shows that toddlers will respond to their distraught peers with caring gestures especially if they had been treated with care themselves. Are these toddlers more highly sophisticated in their moral development than some teen-agers or even some adults? How do you explain this phenomena? One possible variable involved is gender. Gilligan conjectures that girls are more likely to operate from an orientation of caring while boys are more likely to operate from an orientation of fairness and consequently perceive moral dilemmas differently (Bee, 1994). Although research does not support a pattern of behavior differentiation by sex, consider the way young girls play together and the way young boys play together.

Eleanor Maccoby (1990) found that boys are more likely to use a "restrictive style" of play (to limit the interaction partner's choices and thereby ending the interaction sooner) whereas girls are more likely to use an "enabling style" of play (supporting the interaction partner, making suggestions, and voicing support for the partner). Do these same patterns appear in adulthood? For a variety of reasons, men and women predominate in differing professions. Why do females seem drawn to teaching, social work, health care? How are these behaviors related to moral and social beliefs?

What is the relationship between moral judgment and behavior? Are we partially responsible for our development with regard to moral and ethical behavior? Theories of moral development cannot explain all individual behaviors, they can only describe typical behavior of groups. When each of us decides how to behave, there are a number of factors that guide us. One factor is that it is easier to continue behavior we find comfortable than to investigate and consider why we act.

Teachers, social workers, counselors, executives, and health care professionals are encouraged to practice "reflectivity" or the notion of taking stock every so often by asking why they are making the professional decisions they are making. The rationale is that reflection causes us to consider our behavior and modify actions that may have become routine rather than based on the needs of our clients, students or patients. As a parent or a friend, when was the last time you considered why you behave as you do? Is it the way your friends, parents, etc. would have behaved or would have wanted you to behave?

There may be a stronger relationship between moral reasoning and behavior than is apparent on the surface. Does your ability to analyze your behavior relate to your cognitive and reasoning ability? Unless you are a judge or in some other position where your decisions affect others in serious ways, you may take your behavior for granted. Have you ever heard someone say, "I can't help the way I act, that's just who I am." What do you think about that statement now?

Even highly moral persons may choose not to engage in moral actions. There can be a myriad of reasons for this apparent discrepancy. A very moral person may, for example, fail to act on that morality because the situation is so powerful. Even persons who are low in terms of the stage of moral reasoning they utilize may engage in highly moral actions in certain situations. Again, one cannot just measure level of moral reasoning and know whether a person will engage in moral actions without considering at least:

- gender,
- culture, and
- situational circumstances.

esearch uestion

What factors contribute to moral behavior besides level of reasoning?
This has been an important research question in the moral development literature. Findings from moral development research illustrate that to truly understand morality, we must understand:

(a) the individual's level of moral reasoning, and

(b) extenuating variables that may influence the behavior.

(c) Individuals who are moral may not engage in moral behaviors for a variety of reasons.

These reasons include:

1) The person may think that something is morally right to do but not feel compelled to be the person to act.. The person may agree with the reasons that a group has for boycotting a certain restaurant, for example, but not feel obligated to participate in the boycott.

2) The person must assess the costs that are involved in doing something. There are costs involved in engaging in moral actions as well as for failing to take action. When costs are high, the level of moral reasoning is even more likely to predict who will and who will not engage in the moral action.

3) Competing motives might be involved that need to be understood when predicting whether a person will or will not engage in a moral action. Perhaps the person is motivated to become part of a peer group but is required to engage in an immoral act to become accepted.

onclusions

We develop on a continuum in our moral reasoning. In one sense this is much the same as we develop in other areas. Moral reasoning is unique, however, because there are additional factors that guide our actions. Actions may be influenced by a specific situation or by our own levels of self-esteem. We are also influenced collectively by our cultural and ethnic circumstances. Just by living in a western culture, we tend to be strongly influenced by the rewards that come with individual accomplishment and recognition. This part of our social fabric may be changing, however, due to global and androgynous (having both male and female characteristics) influences resulting in increased collaborative and collective reward systems.

 **aper** **opics**

- Behavior is strongly influenced by the adults and later the peers with whom one associates.

  Based on this statement, what conclusions can you draw about the gang behavior that is occurring in the U.S. in Japan and in Great Britain?

  Do you think you would draw the same conclusions if you studied the tribe behavior of non-western countries?

  How are gangs like tribes?

  How are they different?

  What influence does the culture have on the behavior of each?

- What are the ethical guidelines for your chosen profession?

  Usually these guidelines are available through the national association for the given profession. Psychologists, for example, must adhere to the ethical guidelines as published by the American Psychological Association.

  How do these ethical guidelines relate to Kohlberg's levels of moral reasoning?

  What information can you find on what might be done to help persons advance to the level of moral reasoning required by the ethical guidelines of your profession?

 **uggested** **eadings**

Doyle, D.P. (1997). Education and character: A conservative view. *Phi Delta Kappan, 78*(6), 440-443.

Gilligan, C., & Wiggins, G. (1987). The origins of morality in early childhood relationships. In J. Kagan & S. Lamb (Eds.), *The Emergence of Morality in Young Children* (pp 277-307), Chicago: University of Chicago Press.

Jones, E. & Derman-Sparks, L. (1992). Meeting the challenge of diversity. *Young Children, 47*(2), 12-18.

Kohn, A. (1997). How not to teach values: A critical look at character. *Phi Delta Kappan, 78*(6), 428-437.

Staff (1994). Using NAEYC's code of ethics: A tool for real life. *Young Children, 50*(1), 50-51.

Wickens, E. (1993). Penny's Question: "I will have a child in my class with two moms-- what do you know about this?" *Young Children, 48*(3),25-28.

Exercise 1
Moral Dilemmas

Think about the intragenerational family introduced in this text.

Write down as many possible moral dilemmas as you think could occur given the circumstances of the family in this text.

Check with one of your classmates to see if they thought of additional ideas.

Exercise 2
Personal Morality

Think about and write a brief statement that describes what you would like for people in your community, in your profession and in your family to say about you and your morals at the end of your life.

What kind of behaviors would you have to exhibit throughout your life for these descriptions of you to be accurate?

Write a personal vision statement for yourself that puts in writing your goals for yourself as a person, a family member, and a professional.

Check your vision statement periodically to see how close the match is between what you want to do and what you are doing. If the match is not as close as you want it to be, make modifications in your behavior or in your goals.

Exercise 3
Professional Ethics

Our beliefs are based on our experiences as well as what we have learned from others. Imagine that you are a practicing professional in your chosen career. Write briefly, how you would handle the examples given below:

- As a supervisor, you discover that a long-time employee is stealing from the company. You know the employee has a lot of health-related problems. The company does not have good benefits.

    What is your responsibility? What action would you take? Why?

- A friend has shown you the latest piece of software he bought. It is really cool. He offered to loan you the disk so you could copy the program onto your computer. The software comes from a company that makes a lot of money.

    Would you take him up on the offer?

    Why or why not?

Exercise 4
Professional Ethics and the Law

You are a teacher in a day care center. Your supervisor has asked you to tell the state inspector that you never oversee more than 10 children at a time although your typical responsibility is 20 children.

You know that if you reveal the actual situation, your position will be in jeopardy.
You need this job.
You also care about the safety of the children.

How will you handle this situation? Why?

Exercise 5
Life and Death Ethical Decisions

Your aunt who is 97 is in the hospital. The doctor indicates she will probably not survive this latest illness. Your aunt has secretly asked you to unplug her respirator, She wants to die peacefully and with dignity before she deteriorates anymore.

What would you do?

Why?

Exercise 6
Kohlberg's Hierarchy of Moral Development

Analyze your responses to the exercises in this section thus far.

Using your responses as a guide, where do you think you fit on Kohlberg's continuum of moral development?

Does your analysis fit with your perception of yourself?

If it does not, how do you feel about this?

Would you want to change this?

Why or why not?

xercise 7
Ages and Ethics - Kohlberg

Select at least three people to interview of different ages (e.g. a child, an adolescent, and an adult over 35).

- Choose a question such as, If someone tells you a secret and asks you to "keep it confidential," should you respect their wishes, even though you know it is information others should have.

- Predict where you think your interviewee's responses will fall on Kohlberg's moral development continuum.

Person 1: Age: _____

Moral Development Prediction: _____

Person 2: Age: _____

Moral Development Prediction: _____

Person 3: Age: _____

Moral Development Prediction: _____

Pose the same questions to your interviewees and compare their responses. Did their responses coincide with your predictions?

If you were mistaken, what do you think contributed to the differences?

xercise 8
The Role of Punishment

Briefly, write about an incident for which you were punished as a child.

How do you now view that incident as an adult?

xercise 9
Observing Moral Behavior

Observe a group of young children or a group of teens in a group setting related to your profession. Be sure and get permission from a supervisor at this facility before you do the observation.

- What actions did you see that would indicate each persons' level of moral development to you?

- What may be contributing to actions that appear inconsistent with stage theory of moral development?

xercise 10
When I die ...

Write a eulogy for yourself (or someone else if you are uncomfortable using yourself).

- How would you change this eulogy to emphasize characteristics that appear to be important in an "individualistic" culture?

- How would you change this eulogy to emphasize characteristics that appear to be important in a "collectivist" culture?

xercise 11
Studying Moral Development

Consider the moral and ethical issues that you feel are important or challenging in a field would like to study. List 5 that you feel will be important for you to consider.

- Interview men and women in a profession that you think you are interested in pursuing about the ethical and moral issues confronting them.

- Are the issues that you considered similar to the ones cited by practitioners? Were the answers you received different based on the gender of the interviewee?

- With a group of peers or by yourself, find and read the code of ethics for at least three different professions (e.g. nursing, psychology, teaching). Compare and contrast them. What are the critical elements of each?

-

CHAPTER 8
FAMILY, FRIENDSHIPS & LOVE

Each of us, regardless of our background, has experience with family and friends. The family in this text are experiencing several role changes within their family and in their external relationships. How are some of the changes affecting the family in your text similar to changes that have happened in your family or someone you know? Developmental research is aimed at trying to predict the direction these changes might take each of the family members. In addition, research might address what variables (such as personality characteristics, or environmental conditions) that lead to certain outcomes. As an example, Thomas's father is recently widowed. Clearly this change will affect his role in the family. It is also quite likely that it will have an affect on his friendships. If he and his wife had developed friendships with primarily other couples, he might feel uncomfortable being around those friends now. You may also recall from Chapter 5 that changes in roles cause changes in a person's self-concept. All of these complex changes can take place whenever one's status within the family changes.

There are several critical issues surrounding families and the relationships they influence. Activities in this chapter will focus on the changing nature of families, how the environment within the family affects the development of the individual through adulthood, how siblings interact and in what ways your family's patterns of behavior influence your friendships, your decision-making and your parenting behavior. How would your family respond to having three generations under one roof?

 ## Critical Issue - Family Cycles

Families, like individuals, tend to go through cycles and stages. Young families without children focus on different aspects of their relationship, and foster different goals than families in the midst of raising children or who have aging parents for whom they must care. In each of these phases and/or cycles, different family members take on different roles. Although role relationships tend to be fairly stable, there are times within the family cycle that roles can become strained, in conflict and even reversed. Is this true with any of the members of the family in this text?

Susan and Thomas Tran have a family that is experiencing several of these changes in the family cycle. Virginia is suffering the early stages of Alzheimer's. This changes the dynamic of the family and the role that the family members might need to play. The amount of care that Virginia will need will depend, of course, on the speed of her degeneration. But she will have increased needs. In addition, Austin is moving on to college. Susan and Thomas must confront the fact that their children are maturing and approaching the phases in their own lives where they will be significantly less dependent upon their parents.

Can you think of a characteristic discussed in Chapter Six that may significantly affect the ease with which the Trans can adjust to Austin's move to college? How about attachment level? If Austin is securely attached to his parents, he will probably have a smoother transition to college because he has felt compentent to explore his abilities and seek more indepedence in the past. The parents will have already been granting increasing independence to Austin because of their authoritative style of parenting. If, however, a less positive attachment level has been achieved, this change in the family cycle could result in significantly more negative consequences.

Developmental research indicates that the four most influential parental characteristics that influence the success of the parent-child relationship are: (1) warmth (nurturance), (2) responsiveness (communication), (3) level of expectations, and (4) clarity and consistency of rules (Baumrind, 1972). Parents who are warm and responsive tend to have children who are self-assured, confident, hardworking, and caring. Parents who are cold and less responsive tend to have children who are aloof, bitter, angry, aggressive, and lower in self-esteem. Again, it is easy to understand how powerfully such differences could impact families as they experience changes in the family life cycle.

②Critical Issue - The Influence of Environments on Families

One of the most important aspects of families is the way the environment of the family influences growth and development. For example, think about the discipline practices in your family when you were a child. Were the rules strictly enforced? Were the rules applied to all siblings in the same manner regardless of age or gender?

Families with high expectations for their children and who communicate with their children regularly seem to produce children who are more successful in life. But it is not just the degree of expectation that appears to relate to such success. Standards can be set too high and success can be unattainable. Success results when families set high standards of expectation (that are reasonable), help the children to attain such success, and recongnize effort and accomplishment along the way.

Socioeconomic status can profoundly influence the environment of a family. Families that struggle to make ends meet financially are not doomed, however, to have problems. If you look at the list of characteristics of successful parent-child relationships outlined above, you will note that none of these four factors requires a great deal of money. Some families, however, get so wrapped up in their financials concerns (whether it be wondering where money for the next meal will come from or trying to figure out how to make that next million!) that the four characteristics get forgotten.

Chaos and noise can have strong negative affects on people (e.g., Baron, 1994). It seems reasonable to assume, then, that families that live in such environments may be particularly vulnerable. If the family members do not have effective coping skills for confronting and dealing with the negative emotions that can be activated by noise (and especially unpredictable noise), they may be more vulnerable to the stresses that accompany changes in the family life cycle and the typical challenges of being a family.

③Critical Issue - Families Under Stress

Families must deal with stress. It is sometimes difficult for families to maintain an acceptable standard of living without the contribution of more than one family member working. Many families find themselves dealing with divorce, major illness and poverty. Often these pressures are combined producing intolerable strains on family relationships. One result of this is the distressing growth in the number of child abuse cases. When does punishment become abuse? Does it depend on the perspective of the participant?

It is possible that child abuse is more likely to occur at some stages of family life or under certain circumstances. When families are large and parents relatively young and poorly educated, child abuse is more likely to occur (Crockenberg, 1987) Children who are emotionally unresponsive, hyperactive or irritable seem to be more at risk than children who are quiet, responsive and easier to care for (Egeland & Sroufe, 1981; Sherod et. al, 1984). What about abuse of other forms? The experiences of parents as children influence their response to similar situations when they are parents. Individuals who were abused as children, for example, are significantly more likely to abuse their own children than adults who were not abused (Belsky, 1993).

Short term effects of child abuse are seen in toddlers who are unconcerned and less responsive to peer's distress (Main & George, 1985) than toddlers who have not been abused. Long-term effects may be inappropriate and abusive response to peers. Abused and neglected children (and adults) typically tend to be fearful, anxious, depressed and have low self-esteem (Emery, 1989). They are also likely to distrust other people and engage in antisocial or self-destructive behavior (Brassard & McNeill, 1987).

 # Critical Issue - Nature Versus Nurture in Families

How much of your family's influence is due to the environment provided and how much is due to the genes that are passed from generation to generation? In your text, you read about the influence of each of these factors. Which do you think most influenced you? How might you be different if you grew up in a family of a different culture? How would you be the same?

Siblings clearly share genetic similarity. But the similarity in how brothers and sisters think and behave cannot be adequately explained by genetics alone. Family members spend a lot of time together especially during crucial formative years. It is not uncommon for younger siblings to imitate or mimic older siblings. Parents often choose discipline strategies and philosophies that match the ones that were used on them by their own parents.

It is difficult to determine how much of what a family becomes is due to the environment and how much is due to genetics. The link between the two, however, is an important one to consider. Although we do not have an answer to this issue for you, our best piece of advice is to remember learning objective number seven from the introduction to this text. This objective states that, **"Nature (maturation) and Nurture (learning) truly interact."** As a subpoint it was noted that, **"Maturation sets limits beyond which development cannot progress."** This is a crucial point. When considering families, one should remember that the genetic material of each person sets limits of how he or she could possibly develop (one's genes, for example, place limits on eye color that only contact lenses could change). Conditions of the environment, however, influence just exactly how development then occurs within the limits established by one's genes.

Critical Issue - Spending Time as a Family

If families are influential on the development of their children, how much time must they spend with their children? Some mothers and fathers are able and choose to spend more time with their infants. Would the amount of time influence the social and emotional health of children? Remember that there is a difference between the "amount" of time spend with a child and the "quality" of that time. Clearly, adults who spend focused, quality time with their children are more likely to have children who have good social skills, and are emotionally more stable.

But placing a child in daycare does not doom that child to social and emotional problems. Choosing the type of daycare seems to be a very important factor influencing the effects of daycare on children. A daycare that that simulates the positive aspects of a nurturing family can have a positive effect on children (Campbell & Ramey, 1994). High-quality daycare environments that are cognitively stimulating can result in positive effects on both cognitive and social development of children. This is not to say that children spending more time at home will be less cognitively or socially advanced than those experiencing many hours in daycare. The point is, children in daycare will not, necessarily, be negatively affected as many had first thought.

The critical issues that appear to affect the outcome of daycare on children include:

1) the age at which the child enters daycare (children who enter daycare after the first year of life show no consistent attachment difficulties with parents while those who enter during the first year may have difficulties),

2) whether the environment is cognitively stimulating in which books are read, and access to new things is provided,

3) The degree to which the daycare provides access to things that the child is not getting at home. If the daycare environment is less stimulating and nurturing than the home environment then, clearly, the child's development will be thwarted. If, however, the daycare is providing an environment that is as stimulating and nurturing, or more so, than the home environment then the effects can be positive.

esearch Question

Do the attributes of friendship remain constant regardless of the culture? Given the focus of cultures on individualistic versus collectivist ideas, it is possible that cultures may differ in definitions of "friends." There may be a relationship between the play styles of children (recall our earlier discussion of "enabling versus restrictive" styles of play) and the development of friendships. During adolescence, similarity in terms of attitudes, values, and identities become increasingly important in determining who will become friends (e.g., Brown, Mory, & Kinney, 1994) . In childhood, friendships may have been based on very basic physical similarities. Again, this may differ from culture to culture. It is possible that collectivist cultures would encourage friendships with similar others while individualistic cultures might be more willing to tolerate friendships with diverse others.

onclusions

The relationships we have with family members, friends, business associates, etc. are one of the most influential factors in our lives. Moreover, our interactions and responses to these relationships are influenced by our family (or lack of family) history. Family histories are dependent on the factors that describe an individual family's circumstance. For example, the age of the parents, the number of people in the family, the stresses and cycles experienced are powerful predictors of an individual family's history. This history influences the way in which children in the family learn to respond, to communicate and to react to life in general. Despite this strong influence, there is growing recognition that biology plays a greater role in determining behavior and even attitudes then previously thought.

As adults, we make (or will make) crucial decisions with regard to such thngs as how to balance a career and family responsibilities, what relationship to maintain with childhood friends versus new friends, whom to marry (or even whether or not to marry), what our relationship with parents and adult siblings will be. These decisions will be influenced by our family history but also by our culture and what we have learned and experienced as we developed into an adult.

aper opics

1) Consider the intragenerational family in this text. Using information from this chapter and your main textbook. Suggest ways in which the friendships that each of the family members have now and in the future will cause changes in their relationships with each other.
   - What challenges and positive experiences does each family member face?
   - What does the research suggest the family can do to make these transitions as successfully as possible?

2) Does it strengthen or weaken family bonds to have several generations (with their unique struggles) in one household?
   - What does the research literature suggest about this issue?
   - What does the cognitive development research show about the impact of multi-generation households on the cognitive development of children?
   - What emotional development effects might there be?

3) As each person grows and develops, there comes a time when horizontal relationships with siblings and peers become more important than vertical relationships with parents and other influential adults.
   - How do these relationships evolve during the life span?
   - What role does attachment during early childhood play during adolescence and early adulthood development?

uggested eadings

Bivens, J.A., & Berk, L.E. (1990). A longitudinal study of the development of elementary school children's private speech. *Merill-Palmer Quarterly, 36,* 443-463.

Case, R. (1991). Stages in the development of the young child's first sense of self. *Developmental Review, 11,* 210-230.

Caspi, A., Henry, B., McGee, R.O., Moffitt, T.E., & Sliva, P.A. (1995). Temperamental origins of child and adolescent behavior problems: From age three to age fifteen. *Child Development, 66,* 55-68.

Hartup, W.W. (1992). Peer relations in early and middle childhood. In V.B. Van Hasselt & M. Hersen (Eds.), *Handbook of social development: A lifespan perspective.* (pp. 257-281). New York: Plenum.

O'Brien, M. (1992). Gender identity and sex roles. In V.B. Van Hasselt & M. Hersen (Eds.), *Handbook of social development: A lifespan perspective* (pp. 325-345). New York: Plenum.

xercise 1
What is a typical family?

Does the family described in this text fit your idea of a typical family?
How are they similar to and different from your own family?

- Draw your idea of a typical family.
- Ask at least five of your friends to describe what they consider to be their family.
- Compare your drawing to the reports of your friends.

Do you need to modify your concept of a typical family?

xercise 2
Family beliefs and attitudes?

You have a child in the classroom that holds attitudes and beliefs that are quite different from the other children. Based on this, answer the following questions:

How can you allow this diversity within the classroom yet not "force" other students to share the same views?

Imagine that this child is quite militaristic (believing everyone has to follow the rules he has been taught or bear the consequences). What would you do to respond to this?

Imagine that the child is being raised from an individualistic perspective in the home (different needs of children are taken into consideration, punishment and rules are modified to consider these differing needs, and older children have different rules than younger ones). How can you balance this within the context of your classroom?

xercise 3
To spank or not to spank?

The School Board in your community has decided to ban corporal punishment (paddling).

Write a letter to the editor supporting or criticizing the school board for their action.

xercise 4

Describe five variables you can control within a daycare environment that would have a positive impact on the cognitive development of the children.

A parent comes to you and expresses worry that putting the child in daycare will have long-term negative consequences on the child. Using information from this chapter and the appropriate chapter(s) of your main textbook, create a handout you could give to this parent illustrating the research findings on the positive affects of daycare on:

- cognitive development
- social skills
- attachment to parents

xercise 5
The family and the classroom.

As a teacher, why would it be important for you to understand the role relationships a student has within his or her family?

How would these relationships affect a student's:

- learning patterns?
- social and emotional development?
- play patterns in young children?

xercise 6
Day care at the end of the lifespan.

As a health care professional or social service agent, what advice would you give a client on selecting a daycare facility for an aging member of the family?

How might your advice differ if your client was from a different culture?

xercise 7
Love and marriage.

Select a person for whom you currently or in the past had romantic feelings.
1) Write down the loving characteristics you saw in this person.
2) Write down the loving characteristics you think the other person saw in himself/herself.
3) Write down the loving feelings/ characteristics you shared together.
4) Write down the feelings that neither of you were willing to discuss (you may have to do some guessing on the part of your partner).

xercise 8
Who is your dream date?

Write down the characteristics that you would enter into a computer if you wanted to find your dream <u>date</u>.

Write down the characteristics you would enter into a computer if you wanted to find your dream <u>partner</u>.

Once you have done this, complete the following steps as well:

1) How do these two descriptions differ?
2) How are they similar?
3) Do the theories of attraction help explain the differences and similarities?
4) What changes have occurred in society because of computerized dating?

Exercise 9
Friendship

Select three or four people of differing ages.

Interview each of them about their definition of true friendship.

Person Interviewed	Age	Definition of Friendship
Person 1		
Person 2		
Person 3		
Person 4		

Based on these definitions, where would you place each person relative to Piaget's theory of cognitive development?

Person 1: _____

Person 2: _____

Person 3: _____

Person 4: _____

Why did you place each person into the category you assigned?

xercise 10
Classroom roles

If you plan to become a teacher, do you think you will see role patterns develop in your classroom?

How will these role patterns be similar to and different from roles that develop within families?

What might you be able to do to make the development of roles within the classroom as equitable as possible?

CHAPTER 9

ISSUES OF GENDER

You are filling out a form that has two boxes to check after the word
SEX:

☐ MALE

☐ FEMALE.

Is this really what is wanted? Does your "sex" make a difference?

Genetically, although male and female genotypes dominate, there are other combinations of genes that do not fit neatly into either category. Even if genetic sex is straightforward, environmental influences, such as maternal drugs or hormonal levels, can create a mismatch between genetic code and external appearance.

When we use the term sex, we are often referring to gender. Individuals with male or female gender are assigned different social roles, depending on the culture in which he or she lives. Although these social roles are most often assigned in terms of outward appearances, they do not necessarily correspond with the internal world of the individuals.

 Critical Issue - Genetic Sex

Genotype

Genotype refers to the genetic makeup of the individual is by the presence and absence of two types of a pair of chromosomes called the sex chromosomes influences the genotype that determines sex. These two chromosomes, an X or a Y, determine the sex of the individual. An individual with two X-chromosomes will be female and an individual who receives an X chromosome from his mother and a Y chromosome from his father will be male. In most cases, there is one chromosome from each parent. The possibility exists that incomplete division in the creation of an egg or sperm could create gametes (which usually have one sex chromosome) with different combinations such as XX, XY, or neither an X nor a Y chromosome.

When the chromosomes from the egg and sperm are combined at conception there are more than two possible combinations Some of these combinations do not result in a living human being (YO). Others, although very infrequent, are still viable. (Berch & Bender, 1987)

MOTHER (XX)	FATHER (XY)
X	X
X	Y
XX	X
XX	Y
X	XY
X	0
0	Y

Phenotype

The phenotype is the physical appearance or structures created by the genes. The appearance of the individuals with these unusual combinations of genetic code may not be outside of the normal range of characteristics for men and women. Many of these combinations are related to sterility, and many often lead to at least mild problems in mental development. Some combinations also lead to distinctive physical characteristics, such as the webbed neck seen in Turner's syndrome or incompletely developed genitalia.

Critical Issue - Gender Development
Genetics

The genetic structure of XX and XY that is found in most human beings, does not only lead to differences in physical appearance, but also to differences in the way that individuals think about themselves and others. These differences seem to be related to the levels of sex hormones, such as androgen and estrogen, and the sensitivity of the body and brain to these hormones.

Hormones

Hormones are released from endocrine cells in response to genetic structure and environmental influences. The sex hormones encourage the development of primary and secondary sexual characteristics of the physical body.

Hormones in the circulation at particular points in development are also responsible for development of other structures and behaviors. Hormonal levels seem to influence aggression, sexual interest, and spatial abilities throughout the lifespan.

Critical Issue - Gender Roles
Culture

Genetic and hormonal factors partly determine gender but the social environment plays a major role in determining gender-related behavior. Each culture has it's own expectations about appropriate social roles for males and females (and sometimes for the other combinations that appear.) Not all of these roles include positive experiences for the individual. Roles often limit the range of behavior that is displayed and set sanctions for individuals who do not perform as expected. For example: a man is not supposed to enjoy needlepoint as sewing is relegated to women. If a man does sew, particularly in front of others, he is likely to be teased and his masculinity questioned.

To effectively work in a role delegated to the other gender, one must have an uncompromising identity in the appropriate gender (Rosy Greer - the football player and needlepoint designer) or there must be substantial reward for this cross gender behavior (Kaffe Fassett - internationally known textile designer)

Children develop a concept of gender very early a two and one half to three year old can identify others as male or female (usually using hair length and clothing as cues.) By the age of four they understand that girls do not become boys by cutting their hair, and boys do not become girls by wearing a dress. This gender constancy or "conservation of gender" appears at about age five or six. (Marcus & Overton, 1978)

Critical Issue - Masculine or Feminine

 "That's just like a man!"

"It's a girl thing!"

The term personality is often used to describe the unique way in which an individual goes about experiencing and interacting with the world.

While it is possible to group men and women on personality characteristics, the overlap is often more striking than the differences.

While making predictions about the general behavior of a group of men or women on a particular characteristic may lead to differences based on gender, the fact is that what ever characteristic is measured, men and women will both have more or less of the characteristic, depending on the individual. The differences are outweighed by the humanity of both men and women.

Men and women do differ in most cultures. Gender is used to assign tasks and to limit access to resources or behaviors. Since the physical differences between men and women are often very apparent, it is easy to use this cue to create stereotypes about the characteristics of "all men" or "all women."

In American culture, male characteristics have often included those suggesting power and activity while female characteristics are weaker and more passive. Increased awareness in the social aspects of these stereotypes has allowed powerful and active women to emerge just as it has created a place for weaker, more passive males. Even as social changes allow for flexibility in social roles for both men and women, some tasks still are allocated to one gender more than the other. Women still must bear the children (though an individual woman may choose not to do so.) Men still dominate in the work force, particularly in positions that require risk or strength (yet more men are staying home to care for young children while their wives work.)

Research Question

What if you had lived the first 12 years of your life as a girl? With the onset of puberty you began growing a penis and developing the secondary sexual characteristics of a male.

A few genetic males (most live in the Dominican Republic) have a genetic disorder which creates a low level of an enzyme that converts testosterone to DHT (5-alpha-dihydrotestosterone). High levels of DHT appear to be necessary for early masulinization of genitals. At puberty, testosterone levels become high and the testosterone alone is capable of having a masculinizing influence. These "girls" grow up to be normal men with appropriate sexual orientation. (Impersto-McGinley, Guerrero, Gautier, & Peterson, 1974)

How do you think the people you live around would relate to this change?

What seems to be determining the gender identity of these individuals?

Conclusion:

Gender is not a simple concept. It includes the role of genes and hormones, the expression of these as physical and mental characteristics, as well as the effect of culture on learned roles and expectations. This chapter illustrates the combined influence of nature and nurture on the developing individual.

While most people fit easily into biological descriptions of male and female, it is important to remember that there are other possible ways that gender can be expressed in the human body. The incredible variety of the expression of humanity is part of what makes us so interesting.

When psychological and social characteristics are added, human beings become the unique gendered individuals that they are.

Paper Topics

1) Gender roles are an important part of culture. We learn who we are and how we are expected to behave very early on in life.

    a) How did you learn about social roles for males and females?

    b) What were the consequences of playing along versus going against the rules?

    c) Were there conflicting messages from family and friends or school?

    d) Have the rules changed as you have gotten older?

2) How does early exposure to hormones effect brain development and later behavior? Is there a difference in the brains of men and women?

3) What has been done to help people who feel that their gender is inappropriately assigned, that they are a woman in a man's body or a man in a woman's body?
What are the biological implications of this problem?
What are the social implications of the problem?
What are the moral or ethical implications of the problem?

Suggested Readings

Berch, D. B. & Bender, B. G. (1987, December). Margins of Sexuality. *Psychology Today, 21*, 54-57.

Caplan, P. J. & Caplan, J. B. (1994). *Thinking critically about research on sex and gender.* NY: HarperCollins.

Crawford, M. & Unger, R. (1997). In our own words: Readings on the psychology of women and gender. NY: McGraw/Hill.

Davis, R. H. & Davis, J.A. (1985). Chapter 3 - Television's Image of Age. *TV's image of the elderly: A practical; guide for change.* Lexington, MA: D.C. Heath & Co.

Marcus, D. E. & Overton, W. F. (1978). The development of cognitive gender constancy and sex role preferences. *Child Development, 49*, 434-444.

Tavris, C. (1992). *The mismeasure of woman: Why women are not the better sex, the inferior sex, or the opposite sex.* NY: Simon & Schuster

Exercise 1
Your Family and Our Family

Families often divide tasks, with certain family members taking responsibility for a particular task or type of task.

Using the list below, check off the tasks performed by individuals in your family.

In the second table, check off the distribution of tasks that you would expect to see in the Tran family.

Look at your responses in the two tables.
- Where were they similar?
- Where were they different?
- What does this tell you about role expectations in a family?

TASK	Mom	Dad	Bot	Girl	Boy	Child	All
Drive Car							
Laundry							
Cook							
Wash Dishes							
Wash Car							
Vacuum							
Change Diapers							
Home Repair							
Paint House							

TASK	Gene	Virginia	Robert	Thomas	Susan	Austin	Jessica	Kyle
Drive Car								
Laundry								
Cook								
Wash Dishes								
Wash Car								
Vacuum								
Change Diapers								
Home Repair								
Paint House								

xercise 2
Gender Roles

You have many roles as you move between the different aspects of your life. You might be a daughter and a mother, a coach and a team player, an employee and a boss.

List at least ten roles that you play by answering the question **"Who am I?"** ten times.

- How many of these roles relate to your physical body?

- How many of the roles relate to your place in society?

- How many roles relate to your internal reality or sense of yourself?

- How many of these roles carry specific expectations due to your gender?

Write a brief paper listing the roles and discussing how the roles that you accept are influenced:

A. by your gender

B. and by the expectations of your culture ≈

xercise 3
Gender Roles within the Family

Draw a picture of a family. (Do not worry about the skill or accuracy of your drawing.)

1. Describe the roles that people play in this family.

2. How many of their roles are dependent on their gender?

3. How is your family different or the same as the family that you drew?

4. Do you think that families have changed in the last 10, 20, 40, 60, 100 years?

xercise 4
Archival Analysis of Gender Roles

There are many sources of data on gender roles in your culture. Find several examples of any of the following and analyze the gender roles portrayed in them.

A. Magazine advertising

B. Cartoons in newspapers or magazines

C. Folk or fairy tales

D. Children's books

E. Magazine or newspaper photographs

F. Television programs

G. Movies

H. Songs

I. Music videos

Are individuals of one gender more prevalent or more active than the other?

Are individuals portrayed in traditional roles? You might want to find examples over an extended period of time.

Look for changes in the way men and women behave and are treated.

Present your data in a summary report. Use graphs or tables to compare the number of images or examples for each gender and the roles that you observe. You may need to calculate the percentage of individuals behaving in a certain way to make your results easier to compare. Discuss your conclusions.

xercise 5
Gender Role Conflict

Kim (age 16) is the oldest of four children. His mother died three years ago. He took on the role of providing most of the care for the younger children (two girls 3 and 10, and a boy age 5) When his father is out of town on business, he is responsible for the home. He watches the children, feeds them, cleans the house and does laundry. His friends want him to be more involved in school activities. He was the school's most promising basketball player. His teachers are disappointed that he is not getting the good grades that he is capable of.

- Describe the sources of role conflict for Kim.

- What do you think he should do (explain why)?

- What might the consequences be for Kim's long term development?

Choose one of the following perspectives:

Imagine that you are the school guidance counselor. What might you do to help him?

Imagine that you are Kim's teacher. What might you do to help him?

Imagine that you are a nurse working with the local pediatrician. One of the younger children is very ill and Kim brings him/her into the office. What might you do to help Kim care for his sibling?

xercise 6
Individual Differences in Gender

Make a list of terms that are typically used to describe men.

Make a second list of terms that are typically used to describe women.

Draw a line between terms that you think of as being opposites of each other.

WOMEN	MEN
Feminine	*Masculine*

Choose a pair of opposites that you feel distinguish men from women.

Draw a horizontal line across a sheet of paper. Put the word that you consider masculine to the right and the word that you consider feminine to the left. Mark a point on the center of the line to represent an individual with equal amounts of both characteristics or someone who is neutral on the characteristics.

Think of an individual that you know well. Put a circle on the line at the point that represents that individuals ranking on the dimension you are using. Then add a circle for another person, and another. If you feel that two people fall at the same point put one circle above the other on the line. Use a letter or color to indicate men (**x**) and women (**o**). (You may wish to add data from others in your class who used the same dimensions or ask friends and family to add information about people that they know to your line.

Write a brief description of the exercise. Define the terms that you used. Describe the pattern that developed as you identified more people on the line.

Example:

```
                              x
          o               o   x           x
   o      o    x     o     o   x    o      x      o      x            x
```

FEMININE   **ANDROGENOUS**   **MASCULINE**

xercise 7
Activity and Gender Roles

Children learn gender roles through social observation and experiencing the consequences of their behavior. There may also be real differences in behaviors of boys and girls that do not have to be learned.

Are there toys that are preferred by girls or boys in spite of or because of these gender roles?

Observe several children of different ages and genders using the images on the next page. Ask the child to choose between three of the toys.

Record the choice and the age and gender of the child.

1) Does the child display a pattern of responses?

2) How could this pattern or lack of pattern be explained by the point of the child's development?

3) How could the pattern or lack of pattern be explained by the child's sensitivity to gender roles?

Child	Age	Gender	Toy 1	Toy 2	Toy 3	Toy 4	Toy 5	Toy 6
1			N M F	M N F	N N N	F N M	M M M	F F F
2			N M F	M N F	N N N	F N M	M M M	F F F
3			N M F	M N F	N N N	F N M	M M M	F F F
4			N M F	M N F	N N N	F N M	M M M	F F F
5			N M F	M N F	N N N	F N M	M M M	F F F
6			N M F	M N F	N N N	F N M	M M M	F F F
7			N M F	M N F	N N N	F N M	M M M	F F F
8			N M F	M N F	N N N	F N M	M M M	F F F
9			N M F	M N F	N N N	F N M	M M M	F F F

Which toy do you like best?

1.

2.

3.

4.

5.

6.

CHAPTER 10
DYING, DEATH, AND LOSS

This chapter will touch on various aspects of the effects of dying, death, and loss as these relate to four age groups: childhood, adolescence, adulthood and the elderly (older-adulthood). It is of particular importance for the helping profession to have a knowledge of the adaptive or maladaptive grief experiences in order to provide therapeutic assistance.

The older individuals complain of tremendous stress because their traditional value systems may no longer be respected and understood. As a child loses valued relationships or possessions her sense of trust is tested. When loss occurs the child may react by feeling unsafe and insecure. The specific reaction someone will experience in response to loss depends on:

1) the person's developmental level,

2) the assistance and support from others,

3) the cause of the loss,

4) previous experiences with loss, and

5) the cultural and or familial influences of their background.

For example, after purchasing your first car at age 18 you came to value independence, enjoyable rides in the country, the freedom to select the route to work, and the joy of having your own keys in your pocket. At age 76, and because of failing health, the family decides you should no longer drive your car. Because of a previous pleasant experience with retirement at age 67 you determine this loss of independence was to benefit the safety of others. This reaction to the loss of independence was positive.

But what if you viewed retirement itself as an example of lost independence? It is likely that you will then interpret the loss of your driving privileges to be an even greater encroachment into your freedom and independence. Families have to struggle with such losses many times. The cumulative effects of loss can be powerful and devastating if the individual and/or the family do not have adequate and successful coping mechanisms to react to such loss.

Critical Issue - Death, Dying and Loss: Child

If an infant child is hospitalized separation from the parents and familiar environment may precipitate an anxiety crisis with terror. An infant is not really able to understand what death is or what death means. The parent in turn may react to the dying infant with a sense of helplessness. Coleman and Coleman (1985) reported the dying of a child has been perceived as one of the most painful of familial experiences. Marital relationships may experience turmoil. Research has indicated that parents, instead of growing closer to each other during their suffering, experienced an increase in their own difficulties (Yalom, 1989). The family system may feel a negative rippling effect when a child dies.

When the dying child is between the ages of 3 to 6, he or she often has a need to discuss the illness and ensuing death. Friedman (1974) stated that young children have a need to know they will not be abandoned. This ill child, like the infant, may also feel separation anxiety. This child may not always seek to learn his or her diagnosis, but rather, searches for meaningful courage from others in their environment. An ill child's siblings also benefit from knowing what will happen. Following a literature review Share (1972) determined that an open approach in which siblings could show concerns and ask questions allows emotional stability and anticipatory grief to occur when awareness of what is happening is shared.

The loss of a child causes a major emotional change in the family. Members react with hostility and disbelief, especially if the cause is an accident such as a fall, drowning, or a sudden fatal illness. The surrounding factors regarding the death, the role of the child in the family, the emotional and spiritual support the family experiences, and the nature of the relationships within the family will determine the extent of the impact upon the family.

A child aged 6 to 10 years can usually understand that death is permanent and yet they find it difficult to understand they may die soon. If a child becomes ill during this time they may react by being angry. Perhaps this is in part due to the fact they may be unable to participate in "fun" activities. It is difficult for the caregiver to ease this child's anger. The child of this age also has difficulty with abandonment. Abandonment sometimesoccurs when the child is hospitalized in a different town and is without the support of the family.

For the most part, in our society, discussing death with children is not always appropriate. When a pet bird dies, the child may be told various stories to avoid the issue of death or grieving. The child may observe the emotionless parent burying the bird in the back yard. When a family member dies, the death may not be discussed, yet the child observes tears and mourning. The child may not be allowed to attend a funeral or to view the body. Some children may internalize their feelings about the death of a significant person by believing he or she caused the death by angry thoughts or bad behavior and can feel guilty.

Faulkner (1993) stated that a good death could be possible if the family accepts the reality that future time with the ill person is limited. Following acceptance, setting realistic goals for a shortened life expectancy can be achieved. Faulkner reported when the family has been involved in this process there is a positive effect on the subsequent grieving following the death of the ill person.

Any loss experienced by a child can be a traumatic event. Children often lose items that are treasured and trusted. Even the loss of a favorite toy or blanket can be an important event in the brief life of a child. A child may be moved to another community, losing relationships with friends and neighbors, only to experience rejection by the new neighborhood children. A child may lose a pet or a parent by death or divorce. When a person dies, While (1989) reported that "older infants and children experience a sense of loss proportionate to the significance that person played in their lives" (p. 177).

② Critical Issue - Death, Dying and Loss: Adolescent

The adolescent responds to their own dying process much like an adult. The coping mechanisms often observed during the dying process were described by Kubler-Ross in 1969. These five stages have been identified as occurring in adolescents and older individuals. Kubler-Ross (1974) now refers to the reaction to death as emotional tasks. The lonely dying adolescent may react by becoming angry, docile, or noncompliant. It is difficult for them to acknowledge their own death.

When an adolescent experiences the terminal illness of a sibling a desperate need to be involved in the family crisis is experienced. In order to cope with the isolation that may occur Faulkner (1993) reported that children may have, difficulties with keeping their minds on learning, and experience more personality differences between themselves and their friends. Faulkner advised family involvement: "Children react by feeling trusted. They are not left with the frustration of not having had the chance to say good-bye" (p. 136). Being aware of family feelings is critical to the success and progress of the grieving to a rehabilitation process.

When one of adolescent's peers dies, emotions may appear to be out-of-control. Schools react by having counselors available to de-escalate fears, tears, and inappropriate grieving. In order to redirect the distressing emotions careful planning and assessment of interventions by experienced counselors is necessary.

When a parent dies the adolescent's behavior may hide his or her feelings of grief and mourning. It is important for the professional to pay attention to the thoughts and feelings and intervene in a helpful manner.

Adolescents experience other losses than those by death. They may suddenly lose a romantic relationship with either a male or female; lose a friend that needs to relocate with his parents; lose a limb from a freak accident; or lose a close playoff in a State tennis tournament in which he was undoubtedly the favorite for the number one title. In the Intragenerational family, Austin may very well perceive a loss of support and status in his family when he enters college. The outcome of his perception could create an unbearable situation for Austin and failure to survive at college could be inevitable. Even things that may appear to be minor losses can have a substantial impact on the life of an adolescent

Critical Issue Three - Death, Dying and Loss: Adulthood

As we reach adulthood, death becomes a reality of our lives. Bee (1994) reported that research has consistently found mid-life adults to be the most afraid of death. Each year of life increases the potential of death through illness, accidents related to employment and travel, and age. Relationships with spouse, children, and friends increase the possibility of the death of a significant person. The adult's grief and bereavement reactions toward death, dying, and loss are influenced by these lifetime experiences. Additionally, his or her cultural, spiritual, and other emotional life experiences will assist them in the acceptance of either an unexpected or an anticipated loss.

It is during this mid-life period that loss of a spouse is more likely to occur. The sudden death of a spouse may result in physical and mental distress and extreme grieving. The loss of a spouse may create many problems such as: loneliness, insecurity, reduced income, change in lifestyle, and physical symptoms related to anxiety. Many of these same problems are also seen in people who divorce. Both the widow and the divorcee may not have expected, nor prepared for the event.

When the mid-life adult experiences the first death of a parent, the mortality of the self and of the other parent and other loved ones may become apparent. When the second parent dies the adult child may react by feeling forlorn and alone (Murray & Zentner, 1997, p. 649). The adult survivor or adult orphan will need assistance with healthy grieving and bereavement associated with their loss.

While the mid-life adult is experiencing the lessened responsibilities of raising children, the increasing number of elderly parents is creating other responsibilities. The role of the mid-life adult changes to that of being a "parent" to the elderly person. This role reversal can be a stressful experience in addition to the stressors of all the other roles the adult daughter may occupy. This mid-life adult is experiencing many perceived losses at this time.

Critical Issue Four - Death, Dying and Loss: Elderly

More deaths occur in the elderly than in any other age group. Yet, Bee (1994) reports that research has consistently shown that of all the age groups older adults are the least afraid of death. This does not suggest that elderly people do not have needs throughout the process of dying and death. Since eighty percent of deaths occur in an institutional setting and not in a familiar environment (Stanley & Beare, 1995, p. 401) these people may require social, psychological, physical, and spiritual interventions.

As the elderly experience the loss of friends and family their own mortality becomes more of a reality. The loss of their spouse or companion and the inevitable loss of functioning, both socially and physically, threatens their well-being. If the elderly person has displayed positive coping reactions and adept approaches to stress in the past they will be more likely to approach the death of themselves and others with acceptance.

esearch Question

Several studies, as reported by Eliopoulos (1997), revealed higher mortality rates in widowers, especially during the year following the death of their spouse. What might account for this increased mortality rate for the first year following widowhood?

Clearly this is an important issue that warrants further study. Possible research questions include (but are not limited to):

1) Does this mean those widowers who survive the first year of widowhood have more effective coping skills?,

2) What alternative explanations can you think of to explain why a widower might survive for more than a year?,

3) Which professionals may be a part of this man's survival?,

4) How might these professionals impact the length of a person's survival following widowhood?, and

5) How might you go about determining which professionals made a difference?

onclusions

In order for the professional to intervene in a therapeutic manner, knowledge of the age-related reactions to dying, death, and loss is imperative. In order to understand and effectively assist individuals in those situations the professional should discover and develop approaches to provide consistent, respectful, and appropriate regard to all. The focus of this chapter was to provide insight on some matters we will face in one way or another as we experience life and as we practice our professions. The discussions developed in this chapter were meant to be a step in providing such insight.

aper opics

1) Based on information from this text, your main lifespan text, and the lifespan course, when is the best time to die?
   Why did you give the answer that you did?

2) Imagine what you would do to assist Tom (age 14) when a classmate (Sue) informs him that she heard the teachers saying his mother died in a highway accident?
   What could Tom be thinking and feeling?
   How would you intervene with Sue, who is sobbing as she tells Tom what she has heard?
   What are you going to do when Tom's siblings run into the room to see him?
   What are the chances that this may happen in your profession?
   What are your responsibilities in seeing that your interventions are therapeutic?
   Consider a way you could study an intervention to determine its' effectiveness.

3) When someone experiences the death of the last living parent, he or she may be even more effected than when the first parent died. The adult survivor or adult orphan will need assistance with healthy grieving and bereavement associated with their loss.
   How would a facilitator determine the difference between healthy grieving and unhealthy grieving in the members of their support group for mid-life adults?
   Would you gather information from the perception of other family members?

4) Discuss methods for effective coping when someone is terminally ill. Would the methods differ depending on the age of the person who is dying?

5) What communication strategies could be used to explain death and dying to a five-year-old?

6) Pets often have a limited lifespan relative to human life. What can happen when a loved pet dies?
   How might you determine the significance of a pet to a child?

uggested eadings

Bowden, V. R. (1993). Children's literature: The death experiences. *Pediatric Health Care Profession, 19*(1), 17-21, 32-33.

Chesterfield, P. (1992). Communicating with dying children. *Health Care Profession Standard, 6*(20), 30-32.

Forman, S. G. (1993). *Coping skills interventions for children and adolescents.* San Francisco: Jossey Bass.

Gass, K. A. , & Chang, A. S. (1989). Appraisals of bereavement, coping,resources, and pschosocial health dysfunction in widows and widowers. *Health Care Profession Research, 38*(1), 31-36.

Kiger, A. M. (1994). Student health care profesionals involvement with death:The image and the experience. *Journal of Advanced Health Care Profession, 20*(4), 679-686.

Pursell, E. (1994). Physical symptom control in children who are dying. *Journal of Cancer Care, 3*(1), 31-35.

Seale, C. , & Addington-Hall, J. (1995). Dying at the best time. *Social Science& Medicine, 40*(5), 589-595.

Uhlenberg, P. (1996). The burden of aging:A theoretical framework forunderstanding the shifting balance of caregiving and care receivingas cohorts age. *The Gerontologist, 36*(6), 761-767.

xercise 1
Reactions to Loss

Let us take our intragenerational family into consideration as we contemplate the effects of loss.

Make a list of the losses that have been experienced by each grandparent, each parent, and each child. After generating the list of losses, consider and discuss answers to the following questions:

How might the losses of other family members affect each other member of this family?

Do you believe the losses experienced by this family are unusual?

Have you experienced many tangible losses?

Which ones were significant to you or had a significant impact on you? How?

Did others in your family react the same to your losses? Why or why not?

xercise 2
What Does Death Look Like

In this exercise you are being asked to picture death. On a 8 X 11 sheet of paper sketch a picture of what you perceive about death (take no more than about 10 minutes). After you have completed your sketch do each of the following:

Post all pictures in a visible area

Describe your sketch to the class. Allow questions for clarification of your description (10 minutes).

Discuss some common themes reoccurring in the sketches.

How might these different themes affect interventions utilized in caring for patients, family, and friends?

What did you learn about your classmate's perceptions of death?

How might these different themes affect how death would be explained to a preschooler?

How might these different themes affect interventions for an adolescent who has experienced loss by a death?

xercise 3
Personal Loss through Death

Imagine that you have just lost a significant person through death. Your reaction to this loss is very traumatic for you.

Construct some reasons why this loss is difficult for you.

What changes in your life will occur as a result of the loss of this person?

Who will you turn to for assistance or support?

Why did you select this person for assistance or support?

What would you like for this person to do to support you?

xercise 4
Is Death The Same Everywhere?

Most countries and even families have rituals and customs for dealing with death. Consider the following questions about these rituals and customs.

What funeral rituals and customs do your family traditionally consider appropriate and significant?

Would these rituals be different for the death of a child or adolescent?

Are there any rituals you are uncomfortable experiencing?

What ritual would you like to add to the funeral?

What rituals might be utilized for the intragenerational family of Asian descent mentioned in the Introduction?

Exercise 5
Death and Understanding

Much of a person's understanding of death is learned through family's beliefs, family traditions, and cultural values. Think about the intellectual development of the following persons and describe what you would say in response to each of the person's questions.

"Mommy, my hand is bleeding like Lassie's paw when she died. Am I going to die too?" (Age 4)

"Daddy, Tommy said I was going to die. Have I been bad? Can I wake up like Snow White?" (Age 8)

"Health care professional, the doctor will not tell me if I am dying. Please tell me the truth. "(Age 14)

"Teacher, my daddy went to heaven last week. Do you think he misses me? (Age 7)

"My seventeen year old son requires more pain medication for his tumor than I think he should have. " (Mother, age 34)

"What do you mean my husband is dead? I was just down the hall talking to my pastor. Oh, what am I going to do?" (Age 57)

"Son, I realize I have a bowel obstruction, but, I do not want to have surgery at my age". (Age 91)

Exercise 6
Changes at the End of Life

Due to a recent terminal diagnosis Elaine, a 72 year old patient of yours, has been advised by the physician to relocate to a one-room multiple-housing apartment. Elaine appears to have no choice but to move. Elaine states she is too sick to make any decisions and that she is depending on you to assist her. What suggestions would you make to Elaine about each of the following issues? Explain your choices and descriptions.

List ten items you would recommend Elaine take with her.

Elaine arrives at the multiple-housing office where the director states there is only enough room for eight of the ten items. What two items would you advise Elaine to put in storage?

List the feelings Elaine may be experiencing at this time.

What are some of the implications of Elaine having to relinquish her valued items?

What would you observe as Elaine grieves the many losses she has incurred?

xercise 7
Have You Seen Death ?

Discuss your experiences with any or all of the following:

having to care for or support a dying person,

dealing with a grieving friend,

handling a dead body.

Consider how either of these experiences could affect you as an educator. If you have not experienced any of these, what concerns or emotions are you anticipating?

As an educator, how might you prepare yourself for these experiences so you can help students to deal with them?

xercise 8
Facing Your Own Death

You are faced with only three weeks of life remaining due to a fast growing brain tumor. Discuss your responses to each of the following:

List five people you would like to visit with before you ease into a coma.

Write what you would like to say to them, and what you would like for them to say in return.

xercise 9
Values and Dying

Skillful interventions for the dying encompass thoughtful, willing, and careful planning. You have been caring for an 88 year-old woman who, for the last three weeks, has adamantly cried out to die. She is blind, riddled with bed sores, and bed fast. She refuses to go to the health care profession home. She begs you to allow her to take an overdose of her medication. You know that an overdose of her medication will cause her heart to cease beating. Reflect on and respond to the following:

Your *gut* response is to

Your family values say

Society says

Your profession says

Your response is

What would this woman's response be to your response?

An *opposing* point of view to your response would be

This woman's response to the *opposing* point of view would be

Compare your responses with another classmate.

xercise 10
A Good Death!

Interview at least four persons (other than classmates) of varying ages and cultures utilizing the following questions:

1) What is a good death?

2) Describe what you believe to be the death experience.

3) Do you believe religion has a relationship to death attitudes?

4) Do you believe that physicians should address religious beliefs of the dying patient?

5) When should the period of life be lengthened?
   Shortened?
   Unhampered?

6) Are there family risk factors known that have caused death in the family?
   Do you avoid these risk factors? How?

7) If you could select the cause of your own death, what would it be?

8) In the classroom, discuss the collective reactions to your questions.

9) Overall, do all people in a society react to death in the same manner?

10) How might your profession prepare you to be valuable and appropriate when people are experiencing death, dying or loss?

 HAPTER 11

 NTEGRATIVE EXERCISES

These questions are designed to encourage the integration of material from multiple chapters of the text. To develop complete answers, you will also need to use the main text for your course and possibly seek out additional sources of information.

 xercise 1
Giving the Best Gift

Reread the descriptions for each member of the intragenerational family.

Imagine that you have been asked to buy a birthday present for each family member.

- What gift would you buy for each?

- Why?

- Which theories and what information from this text and other sources are helping you make these decisions?

 xercise 2
Greetings!

Go to a store and look at birthday cards.

Look at three or more cards that seem to be designed for people at four different ages (or age ranges).

Based on these cards, what assumptions are being made about development at this level?

Are there any assumptions being made based on gender?
If so, what would these assumptions appear to be?

Given what you have learned about development, how accurate do you believe these assumptions to be?
Some sample words and phrases you might see on cards include:

| over the hill | rebellious | sweet |
| strong | youthful | tired |

xercise 3

How invisible differences affect a life.

A person has just been told that he or she has one of the following conditions.

Choose one of the following problems and answer the questions below.

- Hyperactivity
- Seasonal Affective Disorder
- Borderline Mental Retardation
- Diabetes

What might the symptoms of this condition be?

Consider the impact of this condition and diagnosis on a person.

As you contemplate these effects, answer the following questions:

- How would this have an impact on others (peers, parents, teachers)?
- How would this have an impact on the person's sense of self?
- What effects might this have on school performance?
- How might this affect adult choices (such as career options, whether to go to college, etc.)?

xercise 4
Obesity is more than just being fat

Tom is 40 pounds overweight for his age and height. How might being obese affect each of the following areas of development?:

- physical
- social
- emotional
- self

How might Tom's father (a football coach) react to his being overweight?

How might these reactions affect the same four areas of development?

xercise 5
A Review of Erik Erikson's Theory of Social Development

Match the behavior or statement in column B with the appropriate stage of development from Erikson's theory listed in column A. Write the correct letter in the answer space provided.

ANSWER	Column A STAGE	Column B EXAMPLE
	1) Ego Integrity	A. "Why try I can't do it anyway?"
____	2.) Mistrust	B. "I know you'll cheat on me."
____	3.) Despair	C. "It's my fault he died."
____	4.) Identity	D. "I plan to be a psychologist."
____	5.) Isolation	E. "Yes, I will chair that committee."
____	6.) Generativity	F. "My life has been very fulfilling."
____	7.) Guilt	G. "I don't know who I am anymore."
____	8.) Trust	H. "I aced that test."
____	9.) Industry	I. "I feel so lonely."
____	10.) Initiative	J. "You can borrow my car."
____	11.) Role Confusion	K. "I tied my shoes all by myself."
____	12.) Autonomy	L. "I want to share my life with you."
____	13.) Inferiority	M. "When I die no one will know I'm gone."
____	14.) Intimacy	N. "Here is my annual charitable donation."
____	15.) Shame and Doubt	O. "If I do it, I'll probably mess it up."

Exercise 6
Defining Problems

Match the descriptive statement or behavior in column B with the appropriate disorder listed in column A. Write your answer in the appropriate spacen in the answer column.

Answer	A	B
_____	1.) Anorexia Nervosa	P. Intellectually unable to care for self
_____	2.) Separation Anxiety Disorder	Q. Difficulty maintaining attention
_____	3.) Overanxious Disorder	R. Distorted body image
_____	4.) Attention Deficit – Hyperactivity Disorder	S. Violates rights and rules T.
_____	5.) Bulimia Nervosa	U. Excessive worrying about the future
_____	6.) Conduct Disorder	V. Unrealistic fear of others
_____	7.) Mental Retardation	W. Throws a tantrum when Mom leaves
_____	8.) Avoidant Disorder of Childhood or Adolescence	X. Binges and purges
_____	9.) Autistic Disorder	Y. Excessive defiance and resistance
_____	10.) Oppositional Defiant Disorder	Z. Withdrawn into self

xercise 7
What Type of Development is Involved?

Match the task with the appropriate type of development.

Read each of the following descriptions and place an X **in the appropriate developmental column(s).**

Activity or Description	Physical	Psycho social	Emotional	Cognitive	Moral
Doubles weight in 6 months					
Imitates sounds					
Colors with crayons					
Nail biting					
Follows rules					
Hard of hearing					
Feeds self					
Power struggle					
Bangs objects together					
Demands attention by fussing					
Failure to thrive					
Cooperative					
Attracts attention					
Eats an apple					
Displays fear of strangers					
Vomits secretly					
Pedals bicycle					
Shows displeasure					
Tooth eruption					
Squeals with delight					
Promiscuity					
Feel guilty when violating standa					
Sits alone					
Responds to name					
Menstruation					
Eye-hand coordination					
Hypertension					
Constipation					
Aware of self					

Exercise Answers

Answers for Integrative Exercises -   Exercise 5: 1.) F; 2.) B; 3.) M; 4.) D; 5.) I; 6.) N; 7.) C; 8.) J; 9.) H; 10.) E; 11.) G; 12.) K; 13.) A; 14.) L; 15.) O

Answers for Integrative Exercises - Exercise 6: 1.) C; 2.) G; 3.) E; 4.) B; 5.) H; 6.) D; 7.) A; 8.) F; 9.) J; 10.) I

REFERENCES

Abramson, L.Y., Seligman, M.E.P., & Teasdale, J.D. (1978). Learned helplessness in humans: Critique and reformulation. *Journal of Abnormal Psychology, 87*, 49-74.

Altshuler. J.L., & Tuble, D.N. (1989). developmental changes in children's awareness of strategies for coping with uncontrollable stress. *Child Development, 60*, 1337-1349.

Arkes, H.R., Herren, L.T., & Isen, A.M. (1988). The role of potential loss in the influence of affect on risk-taking behavior. *Organizational Behavior and Human Decision Processes, 42*, 181-193.

Asendorpf, J.B. (1992). A Brunswikean approach to trait continuity: Application to shyness. *Journal of Personality, 60*, 55-77.

Baltes, P.B., Reese, H.W., & Lipsitt, L. (1980). Lifespan developmental psychology. In M. Rosenweig & L. Portor (Eds.*), Annual Review of Psychology* (Vol. 31). Palo Alto, CA: Annual Reviews, Inc.

Bandura, A. (1977). Self-efficacy: Toward a unifying theory of behavioral change. *Psychological Review, 84*, 191-215.

Bandura, A. (1982). The self and the mechanisms of agency. In J. Suls (Ed.), *Psychological Perspectives on the Self* (Vol. 1). Hillsdale, NJ: Lawrence Erlbaum.

Bandura, A. (1986). Social Foundations of Thought and Action: A Social Cognitive Theory. Englewood Cliffs, NJ: Prentice-Hall.

Baron, R.A.. (1993). Effects of interviewers' moods and applicant qualifications on ratings of job applicants. *Journal of Applied Social Psychology, 23*, 254-271.

Baumeister, R.F., Tice, D.M., & Hutton, D.G. (1989). Self-presentational motivations and personality differences in self-esteem. *Journal of Personality, 57*, 547-579.

Baumrid, D. (1971). Current patterns of parental authority. *Developmental Psychology Monograph, 4* (1, part 2).

Bee, H. (1994). *Lifespan development.* New York: HarperCollins. Beidel, D.C. (1991). Social phobia and overanxious disorder in school-age children. *Journal of the American Academy of Child and Adolescent Psychiatry, 30*, 545-552.

Benn, R.K. (1986). Factors promoting secure attachment relationships between employed mothers and their sons. *Child Development, 57*, 1224-1231.

Biling, N. (1995). *Growing older and wiser: Coping with expectations, challenges and change in the later years.* New York: Lexington Books.

Brassard, M.R., & McNeill, L.E. (1987). Child sexual abuse. In M. R. Brassard, R. Germain, & S. Hart (Eds.), *Psychological maltreatment of children and youth.* New York: Pegamon Press.

Braza, P., Braza, F., Carreras, M.R., & Munoz, J.M. (1993). Measuring the social ability of preschool children. *Social Behavior and Personality, 21*, 145-158.

Bronson, G.W. (1972). Infants' reactions to unfamiliar persons and novel objects. *Monographs of the Society for Research in Child Development, 47* (3), Serial No. 148.

Campbell, J.D., & Lavallee, L.F. (1993). Who am I? The role of self-concept confusion in understanding the behavior of people with low self-esteem. In R.F. Baumeister (Ed.), *Self-esteem: The puzzle of low self-regard.* New York: Plenum Press.

Centers for Disease Control (1994). Prevalence of overweight among adolescents - United States, 1988-91. *Morbidity and Mortality Weekly Reports, 43*, 61-69.

References

Colby, A., Kohlberg, L., Gibbs, J., & Lieberman, M. (1983). A longitudinal study of moral judgment. *Monographs of the Society for Research in Child Development, 48* (1-2, Serial No. 200).

Coleman, F. W. & Coleman, W. S. (1985). Helping siblings and other peers cope with dying. *Issues in Comprehensive Pediatric Health care profession, 8* (1), 129-150.

Covington, M.V. (1992). *Making the grade: A self-worth perspective on motivation and school reform.* New York: Cambridge University Press.

Crockenberg, S. B. (1987). Predictors and correlates of anger toward and punitive control of toddlers by adolescent mothers. *Child Development, 58*, 964- 975.

Davidson, R.J. (1992). Emotion and affective style: Hemispheric substrates. *Psychological Science, 3*, 39-43.

Davidson, R.J., & Fox, N.A. (1988). Cerebral asymmetry and emotion: Developmental and individual differences. In D.L. Molfeses & S. J. Segalowitz (Eds.*), Brain Lateralization in children: Developmental implications* (pp. 191-206). New York: Guilford Press.

Egeland, B. & Sroufe, L. A. (1981). Attachment and early maltreatment. *Child Development, 52*, 44-52.

Eliopoulos, C. (1997). *Gerontological health care profession* (4th ed.). Philadelphia: Lippincott. Emery, R. E. (1989). Family violence. *American Psychologist, 44*, 321-328.

Erikson, E. H. (1963*). Childhood and Society.* (2nd. ed.). New York: Norton.

Faulkner (1993). Helping relatives to cope with a diagnosis of cancer in a loved one. *Journal of Cancer Care, 2* (3), 132-136.

Fazio, R.H., Sanbonmatsu, D.M., Powell, M.C., & Kardes, F.F. (1986). On the automatic activation of attitudes. *Journal of Personality and Social Psychology, 50,* 229-238.

Fiske, S.T., & Neuberg, S.L. (1990). A continuum model of impression formation, from category-based to individuating processes: Influence of information and motivation attention and interpretation. In M.P. Zanna (Ed.), *Advances in Experimental Social Psychology (Vol. 23).* New York: Academic Press.

Forgas, J.P. (1991). Affect and social perception: Research evidence and an integrative theory. In W. Stroebe & M. Newstone (Eds.), *European Review of Social Psychology.* New York: Wiley.

Frame, C., Matson, J.L., Sonis, W.A., Fialkov, M.J., & Kadzin, A.E. (1982). Behavioral treatment of depression in a prepubertal child. *Journal of Behavior Therapy and Experimental Psychiatry, 3,* 239-243.

Freiberg, K.L. (1983). *Human development: A life-span approach.* Belmont, CA: Wadsworth, Inc. Publishers.

Freud, S. (1905). Three contributions to the theory of sex. *The basic writings of Sigmund Freud* (A.A. Brill, trans.). New York: Random House.

Friedman, S. B. (1974).The fatally ill child. *The patient, death, and the family.* New York: Wiley.

Gilligan, C. (1982). *In a different voice: Psychological theory and women's development.* Cambridge, MA: Harvard University Press.

Gilligan, C. (1987). Adolescent development reconsidered. *New Directions for Child Development, 37*, 63-92.

Goode, C.B., & Watson, J.L. (1992*). The mind fitness program for esteem and excellence.* Tucson, AZ: Zephyr Press.

Gullo, S. V, & Plimpton, E. H. (1985). On understanding and coping with death during childhood. In S. V. Gullo, P. R. Patterson, J. E. Schowalter, M. Tallmer, A. H. Kutscher, & P. Buschman (Eds.), *Death and children: A guide for educators, parents and caregivers.* New York: Tappen Press.

Hale, C. (1998). *The effect of sibling relationship and birth order on development.* Paper presented at the Butler University Undergraduate Research Conference, Indianapolis, IN.

Henriques, J.B., & Davidson, R.J. (1991). Left frontal hypoactivation in depression. *Journal of Abnormal Psychology, 100,* 535-545.

Hofstede, G. (1980*). Culture's consequences:* International differences in work-related values. Newbury Park, CA: Sage.

Impersto-McGinley, J., Guerrero, L., Gautier, T., & Peterson, R.E. (1974). Steroid 5 alpha-reductase deficiency in man: An inherited form of male pseudohermaphroditism. *Science, 186,* 1213-1215.

Isabella, R.A., Belsky, J., & von Eye, A. (1989). Origins of infant-mother attachment: An examination of interactional synchrony during the infant's first year. *Developmental Psychology, 25,* 12-21.

Isen, A.M. (1987). Positive affect, cognitive processes, and social behavior. In L. Berkowitz (Ed.), *Advances in Experimental Social Psychology* (Vol. 20), pp. 203-253. New York: Academic Press.

Isen, A.M., & Daubman, K.A. (1984). The influence of affect on categorization. *Journal of Personality and Social Psychology, 47,* 1206- 1217.

Izard, C. (1992). Basic emotions, relations among emotions, and emotion- cognition relations. *Psychological Review, 99,* 561-565.

Kagan, J., & Snidman, N. (1991). Temperamental factors in human development. *American Psychologist, 46,* 857-862.

Keesling, D. (1998). *Contemporary attitudes of licensing parents.* Paper presented at the Butler University Undergraduate Research Conference, Indianapolis, IN.

Kittler, M.S. & Sucher, D. (1990). Diet counseling a multicultural society. *Diabetes Educator, 16* (2), 127-131.

Kubler-Ross, E. (1969). *On death and dying.* New York: Macmillan.

Kubler-Ross, E. (1974). *Questions and answers on death and dying.* New York: Macmillan.

Langston, C.A., & Cantor, N. (1989). Social anxiety and social constraint: When making friends is hard. *Journal of Personality and Social*

Lewis, M. (1990). Social knowledge and social development. *Merrill-Palmer Quarterly, 36,* 93-116.

Lewis, M. (1991). Ways of knowing: Objective self-awareness of consciousness. *Developmental Review, 11,* 231-243.

Lewis, M., & Brooks-Gunn, J. (1979). *Social cognition and the acquisition of self.* New York: Plenum Press.

Linehan, M. M. (1993*). Cognitive behavioural treatment of borderline personality disorder.* New York: The Guilford Press.

Lueckenotte, A. G. (1996). *Gerontologic health care profession.* St. Louis: Mosby.

Maccoby, E. (1990). Gender and relationships: A developmental account. *American Psychologist, 45,* 513-520.

Mackie, D.M., & Worth, L.T. (1989). Processing deficits and the mediation of positive affect in persuasion. *Journal of Personality and Social Psychology, 57,* 27-40.

References

Maffeis, C., Schutz, Y., Piccoli, R., Gonfiantini, E., & Pinelli, L. (1993). Prevalence of obesity in children in northeast Italy. *International Journal of Obesity, 14*, 287-294.

Main, M. & George, C. (1985). Responses of abused ad disadvantaged toddlers to distress in agemates: A study in the day-care setting. *Developmental Psychology, 21*, 407-412.

Main, M., Kaplan, N., & Cassidy, J. (1985). Security in infancy, childhood, and adulthood: A move to the level of representation. In I. Bretherton & E. Waters (Eds.), Growing points of attachment theory and research. *Monographs of the Society for Research in Child Development, 50* (Serial No. 209, pp. 66-104).

Marcia, J.E., (1966). Development and validation of ego identity status. *Journal of Personality and Social Psychology, 3*, 551-558.

Marcia, J.E. (1980). Identity in adolescence. In J. Adelson (Ed.), *Handbook of adolescent psychology* (pp. 159-187). New York: Wiley.

McKay, M., & Fanning, P. (1987). *Self-esteem: The ultimate program for self-help.* New York: MJF Books.

Murray, R. B. & Zentner, J. P. (1997*). Health assessment promotion strategies through the lifespan* (6th ed.). Stamford, CT: Appleton & Lange.

Nisan, M., & Kohlberg, L. (1982). Universality and variation in moral judgment: A longitudinal and cross-sectional study in Turkey. *Child Development, 53*, 865-876.

Osborne, R.E. (1993a). Self-concept development and assessment. In *Magill's survey of the social sciences: Psychology.* Salem Press.

Osborne, R.E. (1993b). Self-esteem. *Magill's survey of the social sciences: Psychology.* Salem Press.

Osborne, R.E., (1995). You are what you think: The perpetuating nature of self-esteem. *Proceedings of the Indiana Academy of Science, 104*(3-4), 233-239.

Osborne, R.E. (1996). *Self: An eclectic approach.* Needham Heights, MA: Allyn & Bacon.

Osborne, R.E., & Stites, L. R. (1994). *Perpetuating Low Self-regard: Self- esteem and Interpretations for Success and Failure.* Unpublished Manuscript, Indiana University East.

Otaki, M., Durrett, M., Richards, P., Nyquist, L., & Pennebaker, J. (1986). Maternal and infant behavior in Japan and America: A partial replication. *Journal of Cross-Cultural Psychology, 17*, 251-268.

Pelham, B.W. (1991). On confidence and consequence: The certainty and importance of self-knowledge. *Journal of Personality and Social Psychology, 60*, 518-530.

Piaget, J., & Inhelder, B. (1969). *The psychology of the child.* New York: Basic Books.

Robinson, R.G., Kubos, K.L., Starr, L.B., Rao, K., & Price, T.R. (1984). Mood disorders in stroke patients: Importance of location of lesion. *Brain, 107*, 81-93.

Rosenthal, R., & Jacobson, L. (1968). *Pygmalion in the classroom: Teacher expectation and pupil's intellectual development.* New York: Holt, Rhinehart, and Winston.

Ruff, H.A., Lawson, K.R., Parrinello, R., & Weissberg, R. (1990). Long-term stability of individual differences in sustained attention in the early years. *Child Development, 61*, 60-75.

Savinetti-Rose, B. (1994). Developmental issues in managing children with diabetes. *Pediatric Health Care Profession, 20* (1), 11-15.

Share, L. (1972). Family communication in the crisis of a child's fatal illness: A literature review and analysis. *Omega, 3*, 138-142.

Sherod, K.B., O'Connor, S., Vietz, P.M., Altemeier, W.A. III. (1984). Child health and maltreatment, *Child Development, 55*, 1174-1183.

Smith, S.M., & Shaffer, D.R. (1991). The effects of good moods on systematic processing: "Willing but not able, or able but not willing?". *Motivation and Emotion, 15*, 243-279.

Snarey, J.R., Reimer, J., & Kohlberg, L. (1985). Development of social-moral reasoning among kibbutz adolescents: A longitudinal cross-sectional study. *Developmental Psychology, 21,* 3-17.

Sroufe, L.A., & Fleeson, J. (1986). Attachment and the construction of relationships. In W.W. Hartup & Z. Rubin (Eds.), *Relationships and Development* (pp. 51-72). Hillsdale, NJ: Erlbaum.

Sroufe, L.A., & Waters, E. (1976). The ontogenesis of smiling and laughter on the organization of development in infancy. *Psychological Review, 83*, 173-189.

Stanley, M. & Beare, P. G. (1995*). Gerontological health care profession.* Philadelphia: F. A. Davis.

Sullivan, H.S. (1953). *The interpersonal theory of psychiatry.* New York: Horton.

Tennen, H., Herzberger, S., & Nelson, H.F. (1987). Depressive attributional style: The role of self-esteem. *Journal of Personality, 55*, 631-660.

Thomas, A., & Chess, S. (1977). *Temperament and development.* New York: Brunner/Mazel.

Tice. D.M. (1993). The social motivations of people with low self-esteem. In R.F. Baumeister (Ed.), *Self-esteem: The puzzle of low self-regard.* New York: Plenum Press.

Tomarken, A.J., Davidson, R.J., & Henriques, J.B. (1990). Resting frontal brain asymmetry predicts affective responses to films. *Journal of Personality and Social Psychology, 59*, 791-801.

Tomasello, M. (1993). Infants' knowledge of self, other, and relationship. In U. Neisser (Ed.), *The perceived self: Ecological and interpersonal sources of self-knowledge.* New York: Cambridge University Press.

Walker-Andrews, A.S., & Lennon, E. (1991). Infants' discrimination of vocal expressions: Contributions of auditory and visual information. *Infant Behavior and Development, 14*, 131-142.

While, A. E. (1989). The needs of dying children. *Health Visitor, 62* (6), 176-178.

Wong, D. L. (1997). *Essentials of pediatric health care profession.* (5th ed.).St. Louis: Mosby.

Wylie, R.C. (1974). *The self-concept: Theory and research on selected topics* (rev. ed., 88). Lincoln: University of Nebraska Press.

Yalom, I. D. (1989). *Love's executioner and other tales of psychotherapy.* New York: Basic Books.

Zajonc, R.B. , & McIntosh, D.N. (1992). Emotions research: Some promising questions and some questionable promises. *Psychological Science, 3*,70-74.